SECRET ALBUQUERQUE

A GUIDE TO THE WEIRD, WONDERFUL, AND OBSCURE

Ashley M. Biggers

Copyright © 2020, Reedy Press, LLC
All rights reserved.
Reedy Press
PO Box 5131
St. Louis, MO 63139
www.reedypress.com

No part of this publication may be reproduced or transmitted in any form or by any means, electronic or mechanical, including photocopy, recording, or any information storage and retrieval system, without permission in writing from the publisher. Permissions may be sought directly from Reedy Press at the above mailing address or via our website at www.reedypress.com.

Library of Congress Control Number: 2019952743

ISBN: 9781681062570

Design by Jill Halpin

Printed in the United States of America
20 21 22 23 24 5 4 3 2 1

For Nick, always

SOUTHWEST PIETA BY LUIS JIMENEZ (page 116)

Photo by Ashley M. Biggers.

CONTENTS

ix	Acknowledgments
1	Introduction
2	Good Times and Ghosts?
4	Barely a Dent
6	A Bit of Blocking
8	RIP
10	A Curious Wavelength
12	Early 911
14	Riding in Style
16	Box Top Tales
18	Press Pass
20	Cultural Gold
22	Beneath the Surface
24	Off the Main Trail
26	Does Not Compute
28	The Secret Gate
30	The First Ascension
32	Albuquerque's "Beach"
34	Let's Get Physical
36	Glass Garden
38	Well, Shoot
40	Artistic Fossils
42	Into the Stacks
44	From the Fire
46	Thorny Frosty
48	Rolling Along

50	Nah, I'm Gonna Stay at the Disco
52	Card Reader
54	Gotcha Day
56	With Thanks
58	Family Farmers
60	Flying High
62	Layer by Layer
64	Sun Powered
66	Torpedo Tributes
68	No Longer Starving Artists
70	Blue Plate Special
72	Anthropological Hijinks
74	Still Standing
76	Before the Brand
78	Motor Lodge Mural
80	Midas's Tower
82	Four-Way Stop
84	Giddy Up
104	Fit for a Princess
106	Mile Markers
108	Where's Aldo?
110	Timber!
112	A New Twist
114	Creative Spaces
116	Artistic Intent
118	A Side of Hope
120	Go with the Flow

Page	Title
122	Art Hub
124	No Big Gulps Here
126	Altered States
128	You're Going to Need More Clamps for That
130	To the Wall
132	Written in Stone
134	Skating Along
136	Movie Memories
138	A Suburb of One's Own
140	Coming Home
142	Cheers to Prohibition
144	A Sight to Behold
146	Gone but Not Forgotten
148	Parq It
150	Stuffed
152	Craning to See
154	Burgers and Thrift Store Finds
156	Going Green
158	Glass House
160	Forgotten Village
162	Mountain Memorial
164	Math Aloft
166	Taco Tuesdays, Sopaipilla Saturdays
168	Slithering Sights
170	Loco for Locomotives
172	Puck Drop
174	Duke City's Doge

176	Cultural Nexus
178	A Different Kind of Cleanse
180	That's a Stretch
182	Chiseling History
184	Lucy, We've Got a Star
186	Generations of Genízaro
188	Universal Views
190	Martineztown Monument
192	Winging It
194	Our Lady of the Tree
196	Settlers and Sopaipillas
198	High Notes
200	Sources
211	Index

ACKNOWLEDGMENTS

Writing a book of this nature takes a village—a group of people who overheard an urban legend, noticed an offbeat location, or inquired about a destination Albuquerqueans walk by every day without knowing its history. I appreciate these curious residents who shared their particular knowledge, as well as their ideas: Jesse Heron, proprietor of Painted Lady Bed and Brew; Dr. Matthew Schmader, who has studied Piedras Marcadas Pueblo for decades; and Thea Haver and Ethan Aronson, of Modern Albuquerque.

Thank you to Mike Coltrin, who took an impromptu hike to TWA Canyon for a photo assist.

I also extend my thanks to individuals who helped me in my search of secret Albuquerque. These guides include Jim Walther, of the Nuclear Science and History Museum; Sara Dell, member of the First Unitarian Church; Greg Morrison, of the American Society of Radiology Technologists; Tom Baker, of the Telephone Museum of New Mexico; Steve and Kara Grant, of the Downtown Historic Bed & Breakfast, Laura Dunagan, of the Albuquerque Press Club; Elizabeth Stone, of the Gutierrez-Hubbell House; Steve Richey, volunteer at the Petroglyphs National Monument; Matthew Peterson, of Albuquerque Open Space; Kevin Troutman, of AMAFCA; Carla Sinopoli, of the Maxwell Museum of Anthropology; Leba Freed, of the Wheels Museum; Ashley Fathergill, of YogaZo; Oma; Ellen Babcock, of Friends of the Orphan Signs; Marilee Nason, of the Anderson Abruzzo International Balloon Museum; sheri crider, of the Sanitary Tortilla Factory; Matt DiGregory, of the Range Café; Joe Sabatini and Roland Penttila, of the Albuquerque Historical Society; architect

Bart Prince; Greg Morris and Julie Yung, of Hope Café; Larry D. Parker, of the KiMo Theater; Janet deVesty, of the Unser Museum; Angie Poss and Dr. David Eck, of the New Mexico State Land Office; Katie Jurney, of Albuquerque Roller Derby; Hugh Hacket, of Maggie's Diner; Jonathan Wolfe, of the Fractal Foundation; Mike Hartshorne, of the NMSL&RHS; Johnny Goodwin and Ken Carson, of Nexus Blue Smokehouse; and professor Moises Gonzales.

Nearly last, though never least, thank you to my husband, Nick Cessac, who is my adventure partner and sounding board. He also shot a fair number of the photos you'll see in these pages.

Finally, a heartfelt thanks to the City of Albuquerque. Thank you for never failing to surprise me.

INTRODUCTION

When I penned *100 Things to Do in Albuquerque Before You Die*, now in its second edition, a few items came across my desk that were simply too offbeat to include in that introductory guide. My collection of outtakes formed the early list of oddities and obscurities for *Secret Albuquerque*, which explores the hidden histories behind well-known places and off-the-radar destinations.

As I began learning more about these items—a mysterious eye painted on a boulder in the Sandia Mountains, a former bootlegger's bar, a famous rock and roll front man's childhood home—I realized I wasn't researching disparate pockets of eccentricities. I was telling Albuquerque's story. It's a multi-cultural city whose people defy easy categorization. A place where spies, scientists, tarot card readers, creatives, record-setting athletes, thought leaders, and railroad enthusiasts were and are neighbors. A city whose more than three-hundred-year-long chronicle turns every building into a history vault. A city where unexcavated Pueblos (and occupied ones) and Spanish Colonial homes are just a few blocks away from modern architecture marvels. A city where Route 66 motor lodges aren't relics and where artists never fail to surprise.

This book is a discovery roadmap that will guide you to every corner of the greater Albuquerque area, from Los Lunas to the East Mountains and many neighborhoods in between. Whether you're a visitor or a long-time resident, I hope that whenever you open *Secret Albuquerque*, you'll uncover a new place to visit, or to revisit with deeper understanding. I hope you use it to tackle weeknight excursions or to inspire Sunday drives. More than anything, I hope it helps you see Albuquerque as it is: endlessly fascinating.

GOOD TIMES AND GHOSTS?

Where can you stay the night in a former brothel?

If the walls of a humble adobe in Wells Park could talk, they would tell sordid tales of buried money, moonshiners, and knife fights. As early as 1904, the building operated as the Swastika Saloon and advertised its "wine room in connection"—code to those in the know that a brothel was on site. With the predominantly male workforce at the American Lumber Company just across the street and the citywide population made up of five men to every woman, the brothel business thrived. It's thought that the brothel operated into the middle of the twentieth century, well past when prostitution was made illegal.

By the time Jesse Herron, co-owner of the Albuquerque Tourism & Sightseeing Factory, purchased the building in 2014, it was a neighborhood eyesore. He brought the crumbling building back to life as the Painted Lady Bed & Brew. It officially opened in 2018. Proclaiming that breakfast is overrated, this B&B provides guests with two servings of craft beer each evening. Most of the cans and bottles come from nearby craft breweries, testifying to the Painted Lady's admirable location in a brewery hop-bed—and that's truly saying something because Albuquerque

---

> The Painted Lady Bed & Brew is the first and, as of this writing, the only bed and brew in the state.

Before it was a bed-and-brew, Painted Lady was a saloon with a "wine room"—a.k.a. a brothel. It's been fully renovated with period and unique details. Photos courtesy of Painted Lady Bed & Brew.

PAINTED LADY BED & BREW

What: Not your grandma's B&B

Where: 1100 Bellamah Ave. NW

Cost: From $130 per night

Pro Tip: Ask the proprietor if you may step inside the vintage "Alburquerque" trolley on site.

overflows with suds. Herron kept original building details where possible, from doors and gates to the nineteenth-century floors in the suite named after Albuquerque's most infamous madam, Lizzie McGrath.

He also kept the haint-blue beadboard ceilings. The traditional color for Southern porch ceilings is thought to ward off evil spirits. It's a good precaution because, with nearly 140 years of history in this building, there are bound to be a few guests who never checked out. Herron has several ghost tales to share, from friendly spectral voices asking if they can have a beer, to more malevolent spirits who didn't take kindly to their eviction notices. You can ask him about these ghost tales over an evening beer.

BARELY A DENT

Why does Albuquerque have "Broken Arrows"?

The U.S. Armed Forces refer to a nuclear weapon accident that falls short of threatening war as a "Broken Arrow." According to the Department of Defense, there have been thirty-two such incidents since the first occurred off the coast of British Columbia in 1950. New Mexico has had two occurrences, including one near Kirtland Air Force Base on May 22, 1957.

On that day, a B-36 was transporting a forty-one-thousand-pound Mark 17 thermonuclear bomb from Biggs Air Force Base, near El Paso, Texas, to Kirtland Air Force Base. The plane was at an altitude of 1,700 feet, just south of Albuquerque's airport (and Kirtland), when the explosive dropped through the bomb bay—taking the doors with it. Luckily for Albuquerque, the weapon did not have a nuclear capsule. However, it did have a highly volatile component. The explosion created a crater about twenty-five feet across and twelve feet deep, and it scattered debris as far as a mile from the impact point.

The National Museum of Nuclear Science & History doesn't have that particular weapon, but it does have two from a 1966 Broken Arrow in Palomares, Spain. The

---

THE NATIONAL MUSEUM OF NUCLEAR SCIENCE & HISTORY

What: The country's national museum for the Atomic Age

Where: 601 Eubank Blvd. SE

Cost: From $12 for adults

Pro Tip: Many of the museum docents are retired veterans; ask them about their own military service.

Broken Arrows are nuclear accidents that don't result in nuclear war. Albuquerque has had an incident, but these shells are from an event in Palomares, Spain. Photos by Ashley M. Biggers.

scratched, dented, and crumpled bomb casings are reminders of just how close the world has come to nuclear incidents on several occasions.

A B-52 was carrying four nuclear bombs when it collided with a KC-135 while refueling over Palomares, Spain, in 1966. The bombs fell, and one landed in the sea while three landed on the ground. Of those that landed on the ground, two detonated and released radioactive materials.

A BIT OF BLOCKING

Why did a world-famous designer create a mural in an Albuquerque church?

Designer Alexander Girard (1907–1993) was famous for designing everything from Braniff International Airways' sugar packets to planes, and everything from the matchbooks to the tableware at Manhattan restaurant La Fonda del Sol. He also created trends as a Herman Miller textile designer. In Santa Fe, he's best known for donating the foundational collection of the Museum of International Folk Art. In other words, he's not known for being a Duke City muralist. But the massive mural he made for Albuquerque's First Unitarian Church sanctuary ranks among his most impressive works.

Girard was friends and colleagues with architect Harvey Hoshour, who designed several of Albuquerque's modernist landmarks. Hoshour designed the 1964 sanctuary building where the mural was to be installed and turned to Girard to create the centerpiece. It stood in Hoshour's building for decades; however, when the congregation outgrew the original sanctuary in 2013, it painstakingly removed and reinstalled the mural wood block by wood block. The mural is made up of five thousand three-by-three-inch wood squares. The

---

Girard scavenged northern New Mexico villages for materials. He used only found, scrap wood. Each wood block is its original color; none were stained or painted to fit the composition.

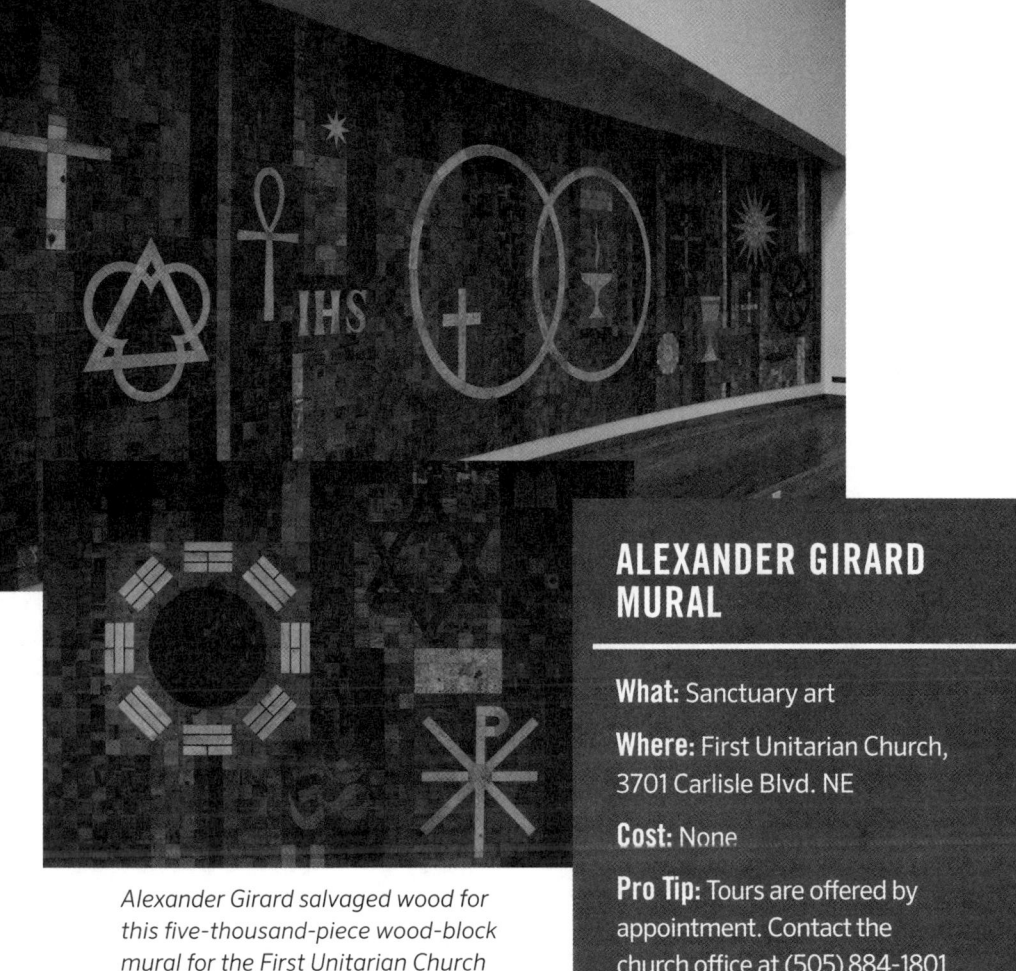

Alexander Girard salvaged wood for this five-thousand-piece wood-block mural for the First Unitarian Church sanctuary. The mural features symbols of the world's religions. Photos by Ashley M. Biggers.

ALEXANDER GIRARD MURAL

What: Sanctuary art

Where: First Unitarian Church, 3701 Carlisle Blvd. NE

Cost: None

Pro Tip: Tours are offered by appointment. Contact the church office at (505) 884-1801 to arrange a visit.

process took three months and wasn't finished until a missing block was rediscovered in a desk drawer just in time for the dedication ceremony.

Girard's mural stretches eight feet high and spans forty feet across the back of the sanctuary's curved wall. Unitarians are known for living not by a creed but by a covenant, so the mural honors the world's major and minor religions and spiritual practices. The Buddhist Dharma Wheel floats in the same field as an Islamic star and crescent. The symbol of Unitarianism, a flaming chalice, is set off center, while a cross (Girard was Catholic) sits dead center.

RIP

Why does a fictional character have a real-life gravestone?

Breaking Bad mania hit fever pitch shortly before the series finale on September 29, 2013. And Albuquerque, where the show was filmed and set, was no exception. (Spoiler alert!) After the show's central character—chemistry teacher turned meth kingpin Walter White—met his dramatic end, fans purchased an obituary in the city's paper of record, the *Albuquerque Journal*.

Around two hundred fans/mourners gathered at Sunset Memorial Park on Saturday, October 21, 2013, to lay White to rest. The service began with an eighty-car-deep funeral procession down Second Street that included a Bounder RV. The show made this RV style famous by turning it into a mobile meth kitchen. Former *Breaking Bad* set decorator Michael Flowers led the service, which benefited Albuquerque Health Care for the Homeless.

Local restaurant Vernon's Speakeasy set up the charity endowment fund and purchased a gravestone for White, which it intended to install at the cemetery. However, more than a thousand family members of the real-life people laid to rest at Sunset Memorial Park signed a petition protesting White's grave marker. Instead, organizers

---

More than six years after the show's last episode, fans from around the globe still come to Albuquerque to see *Breaking Bad* filming locations in real life.

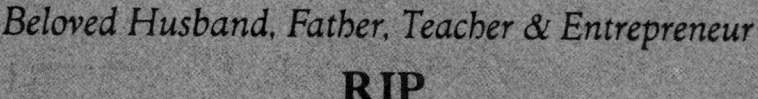

Breaking Bad's *Walter White* has a real-life gravestone at an Albuquerque strip mall. Photo by Ashley M. Biggers.

WALTER WHITE'S GRAVESTONE

What: *Breaking Bad* fan mecca

Where: The Village Shops at Los Ranchos, 6855 Fourth St. NW, Los Ranchos de Albuquerque

Cost: None

Pro Tip: Toast White's death with a drink at Vernon's Speakeasy, a "hidden" steakhouse.

set it in a stucco wall at the Village Shops at Los Ranchos, just across from Vernon's Speakeasy. A bench sits next to the gravestone—a place, perhaps, to contemplate how the milquetoast character transformed into an outlaw.

A CURIOUS WAVELENGTH

How did a famous criminologist's X-ray table land in the Duke City?

Affordable land brought the American Society of Radiologic Technologists headquarters to the Duke City in 1984. The professional society of medical imaging and radiation therapy professionals toted a grandma's attic worth of archives with it—and solicited many more for the 2005 opening of the ground-floor museum. Among these is a 1920s Engeln Electric/Victor Bucky Diaphragm Table collected from the workshop of criminologist William Harper, who is most famous for his expert testimony in the trial of Senator Robert F. Kennedy's assassin, Sirhan Sirhan.

The museum chronicles X-ray technology's development, beginning with Wilhelm Conrad Röntgen's 1895 discovery in Germany, when he observed a fluorescent glow while working with a cathode-ray tube. Moving beyond discovery, the exhibits display early tubes and X-ray machines in the field. The museum also honors those who gave their lives during the technology's early

---

The American Society of Radiologic Technologists Museum also displays items technicians have seen on X-rays inside human bodies, including eyeglasses, pliers, and toy soldiers, among other rather uncomfortable-sounding items.

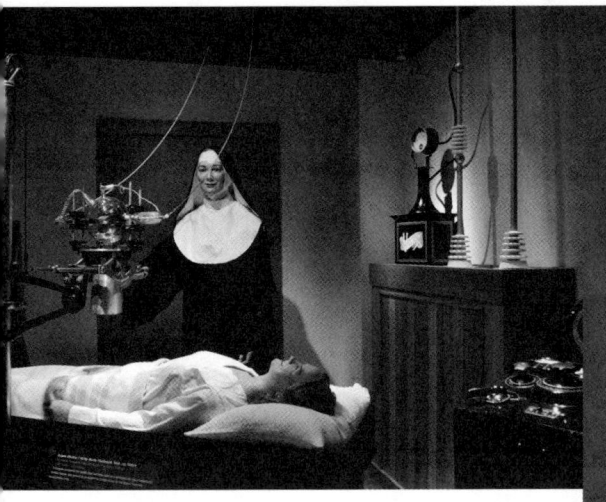

This X-ray table came from the workshop of criminologist William Harper. Photo by Ashley M. Biggers.

development. Clarence Dally, for example, was a glass blower in Thomas Edison's laboratory who died from skin cancer as a result of repeated X-ray exposure. His death led Edison to abandon his X-ray research.

Greg Morrison, associate executive director of ASRT, says the profession has been dominated by women, and the museum reflects that. Marie Curie's research was instrumental in bringing medical imaging to the front lines during World War I so soldiers could be treated in the field. Nuns, who were often medical caregivers, also impacted the profession through their work in Catholic hospitals. Sister Mary Beatrice was one of the first registered technologists.

Dioramas bring imaging technology to life; a nun mannequin representing Sister Mary Beatrice stands over Harper's table. The museum also honors today's technology and practitioners. As Morrison observes, "A good technologist is like an artist."

AMERICAN SOCIETY OF RADIOLOGIC TECHNOLOGISTS MUSEUM AND ARCHIVES

What: An X-ray geek's paradise

Where: 15000 Central Ave. SE

Cost: None

Pro Tip: Schedule a tour with Greg Morrison. Many of the artifacts are from his personal collection.

EARLY 911

Where is the switchboard used to call for help during Pancho Villa's New Mexico raid?

Telephone operator Susan Parks may not have been able to connect to emergency services in the early hours of March 9, 1916, but she knew whom to call when 485 Mexican revolutionaries led by General Francisco "Pancho" Villa rode on the small town of Columbus, New Mexico. As she shielded her infant from flying glass and sustained an injury herself, she connected to a Deming operator. That operator sent troops to the aid of Camp Furlong soldiers outside Columbus. Villa was seeking food, clothes, and munitions for his shrinking band of revolutionaries in the sleepy and unsuspecting town of Columbus, just a couple of miles over the border from Mexico. The revolutionaries set fire to the town, causing residents to flee or shelter in the Hoover Hotel, where the telephone switchboard stood. Thanks in part to Parks's call, General John J. Pershing and thousands of U.S. troops reached Columbus just days after the raid, launching an ultimately unsuccessful search for Villa in Mexico. Now that bullet-hole-marked switchboard resides in the Telephone Museum of New Mexico.

TELEPHONE MUSEUM OF NEW MEXICO

What: Historical switchboards and headsets

Where: 110 Fourth St. NW

Cost: None

Pro Tip: Hours are limited, so call ahead to ensure the museum is open.

The Telephone Museum of New Mexico houses historical headsets, switchboards, and memorabilia. Photo by Ashley M. Biggers.

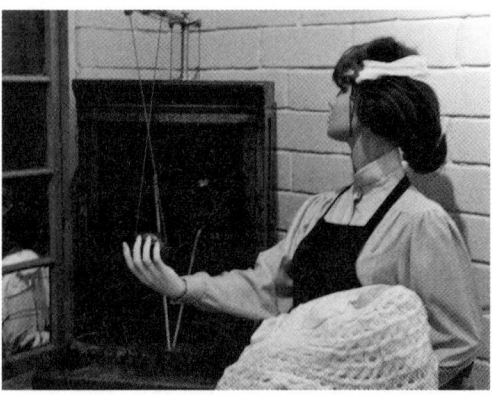

This switchboard was used to call for help when General Francisco "Pancho" Villa rode on Columbus in 1916. The Telephone Museum of New Mexico re-creates the scene with operator Susan Parks. Photo by Ashley M. Biggers.

The museum houses a telephone-artifact trove, including early and unusual headsets—Elvis phone, anyone? It displays switchboards used across New Mexico, such as one used in Tucumcari from 1952 to 1963. Longtime AT&T employee Tom Baker and his wife run the museum. They lease the building from the telephone company. The museum has several artifacts reflecting the telecom giant's history, too, such as a two-thousand-pound cast-bronze medallion from the American Telephone & Telegraph Co. The seven-foot-diameter medallion was removed from the company's New York City office in 1984 when AT&T broke up. It retired to New Mexico along with the savvy executive who was able to procure it from the building.

The museum is housed in a 1906 building that was the original home of the Colorado Phone Company in New Mexico. Why not the New Mexico Phone Company? Because the state was still a territory at the time.

RIDING IN STYLE

How did J. Robert Oppenheimer's limo drive into a local museum?

How did Manhattan Project scientists travel from their secret city in Los Alamos, New Mexico, to the nuclear weapon test site near Alamogordo? In style, of course. A retrofitted limousine transported passengers including the Manhattan Project's scientific director and nuclear physicist J. Robert Oppenheimer, who is considered the father of the atomic bomb. That vehicle is now parked at the National Museum of Nuclear Science & History.

It started its life in the Detroit, Michigan, Packard plant. It was originally a Clipper Six model and was built between August 1941 and February 1942. The Packard was sent to the Fitzjohn Coach Company in Muskegon, Michigan, where it was converted into a limo with a six-foot stretch of wood. After its life working for the Manhattan Project, the limo was lost for many years. Historians discovered it in 2005, in a Gallup, New Mexico, salvage yard owned by Dan Dolan. He donated it to the museum, where it underwent an extensive restoration.

The National Museum of Nuclear Science & History houses numerous nuclear-age artifacts like this one. In

---

The National Museum of Nuclear Science & History is the only congressionally chartered museum on the topic.

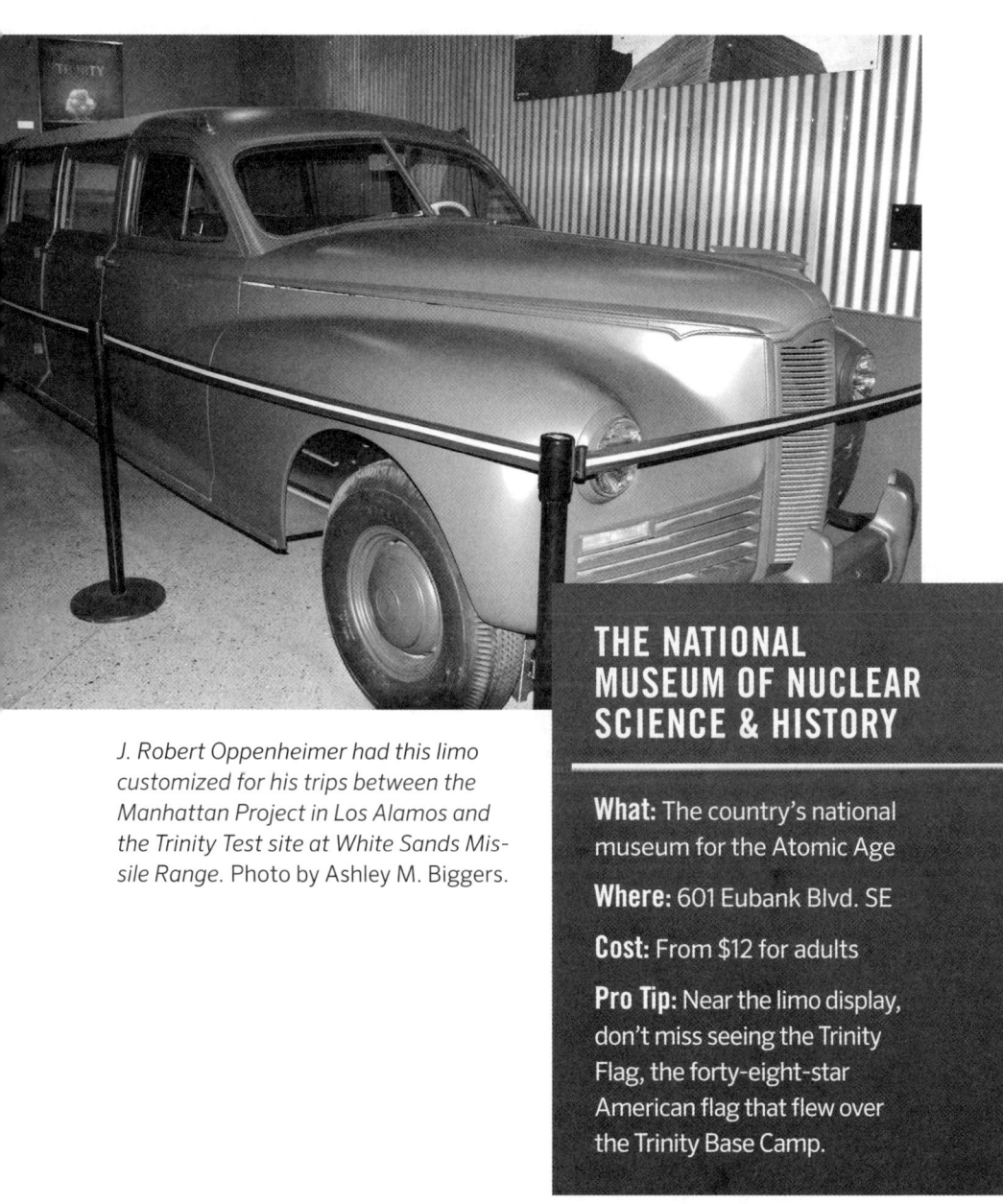

J. Robert Oppenheimer had this limo customized for his trips between the Manhattan Project in Los Alamos and the Trinity Test site at White Sands Missile Range. Photo by Ashley M. Biggers.

THE NATIONAL MUSEUM OF NUCLEAR SCIENCE & HISTORY

What: The country's national museum for the Atomic Age

Where: 601 Eubank Blvd. SE

Cost: From $12 for adults

Pro Tip: Near the limo display, don't miss seeing the Trinity Flag, the forty-eight-star American flag that flew over the Trinity Base Camp.

the exhibits, the limo sits near the Fat Man atomic bomb—a casing identical to the prototype tested in the New Mexican desert on July 16, 1945, ushering in the Atomic Age.

BOX TOP TALES

Why is a bed and breakfast known as the Spy House?

One of the biggest espionage incidents in U.S. history occurred in an unassuming Arts and Crafts-style home in the Huning Highland neighborhood. On June 2, 1945, Soviet courier Harry Gold appeared on the doorstep of the Freeman boarding house where Manhattan Project machinist David Greenglass and his wife, Ruth, lived. During the week, Greenglass worked in Los Alamos, where the nuclear bomb was being developed. On weekends, he joined his wife in their Albuquerque apartment. Greenglass's sister, Ethel Rosenberg, and her husband, Julius, had convinced Greenglass to spy and pass drawings of the nuclear weapon's trigger mechanism to the Soviets through a courier.

On the day of the exchange, Gold and Greenglass matched pieces cut from a Jell-O box to verify they had the right individual. Then, Greenglass handed over the information for $500. (Ruth Greenglass is said to have purchased a war bond with part of the payment, patriots that they were.) Within a few days, the information was in Soviet hands.

In 1951, Greenglass provided evidence against the Rosenbergs in their espionage trial. In part because of

---

The Greenglass room includes a small, simple table where the spy sketched the atomic bomb's trigger mechanism. The table was used as evidence during Ethel and Julius Rosenberg's trial.

Soviet spy David Greenglass lived at this home—and passed drawings of nuclear weapons to a currier here in 1945. Photo by Ashley M. Biggers.

Greenglass's testimony, the Rosenbergs were sentenced to death by electric chair. They died June 19, 1953. Greenglass, who had made a plea bargain, served prison time and lived out his life under an assumed name.

Today, visitors can check into the home where this historic exchange took place. The Spy House is part of Downtown Historic Bed & Breakfast, an accommodation that spans five historic buildings. Innkeepers Steve and Kara Grant purchased the Spy House in 2001 as a flip house, but they soon fell in love with its history and elegant 1912 details. They began restoring neighboring properties and, in 2008, opened them collectively as a bed and breakfast. The Grants kept as much original detail as possible, especially in the #4 room and kitchenette where the Greenglasses lived. The table where Greenglass sketched the nuclear weapon's mechanisms is still in the room today.

DOWNTOWN HISTORIC BED & BREAKFAST

What: The Spy House

Where: 209 N. High St. NE

Cost: From $149

Pro Tip: If you can't stay in the Greenglass room, you should instead book the carriage house. The charming building was indeed where horses and carriages were kept when the home was built in the early twentieth century.

PRESS PASS

Why is there a log cabin in the middle of Albuquerque?

The log-cabin-style home perched on a hill in East Downtown is a Duke City rarity. Architect Charles Whittlesey built the three-story family home in 1903. Whittlesey, chief architect for the Santa Fe Railroad, chose the location so he could oversee construction of the Alvarado Hotel. Whittlesey's railroad connections enabled him to bring in the logs necessary for the Norwegian villa's facades. The Whittlesey family resided there as late as 1908. Over the following decades, various people and entities owned the home. Each modified it to his/her/their unique needs. It evolved into a maze of offices, poker rooms, and basement lounges. The house's main room, with a lava rock fireplace, built-in bookcases, and grand log-beam ceiling, is largely original. One notable owner was an Albuquerque railroad hospital (now Hotel Parq Central, see page 148) nurse, Clifford Hall, who convinced her then-suitor and later husband Arthur B. Hall to purchase the house in 1920; she came to own the house and lived there over the next forty years.

The Albuquerque Press Club purchased the Whittlesey House in the 1970s. The member-owned private club

---

When Whittlesey built his home, he was literally overseeing the Alvarado Hotel construction. He could see it from his house on the hill.

The Albuquerque Press Club is housed in the Whittlesey House, a log cabin perched in the middle of the Duke City. Photo by Ashley M. Biggers.

operates a bar and gathering space there. The press club claims around 240 members, some of whom are professional members of the press and others who are social (non-press) members. According to president and membership chair Laura Dunagan, many members join simply for a public place to smoke inside—a rarity at most other bars and clubs around town, and an oft-debated subject even here. Regardless of their reasons, the members are usually rewarded with a *Cheers*-like, everybody-knows-your-name vibe and thoughtful conversations with other members, who are often "outside what passes for normal, but in really interesting ways," Dunagan says. Though the club operates independently of the Whittlesey House Preservation Foundation, Press Club members have lovingly adopted the house and assisted with its upkeep over the years.

ALBUQUERQUE PRESS CLUB

What: Quirky private membership club

Where: 201 Highland Park Cir. SE

Cost: Memberships from $30

Pro Tip: Only members and guests of members are allowed inside. If you drop in, you may be able to find a member who will sign you in. If you want to be sure of entrance, contact the club ahead of time to arrange a tour.

CULTURAL GOLD

Does Albuquerque have buried treasure?

Dating to 1860, the Gutiérrez-Hubbell House was the home of Juliana Gutiérrez, a descendant of some of the wealthiest and most powerful families in New Mexico. Seeking to ensure their family's connections to the new territorial power (a.k.a. the United States), her father engineered her marriage to James Lawrence "Santiago" Hubbell, a Connecticut man with entrepreneurial aspirations. The building was not only their family home but also a mercantile, trading post, stagecoach stop, and post office.

The home was prone to raids; it was the last place in Albuquerque attacked by Comanches in the 1880s. To protect their flourishing earnings, the Hubbells were said to have buried gold on the property. It was the territorial equivalent of burying a coffee can of money or tucking cash into your mattress. Despite members of the public occasionally showing up with metal detectors to scour the grounds, searches haven't turned up any evidence of treasure.

The true treasure may be the family and home's lasting influence. John "Lorenzo" Hubbell, the second of

---

Situated along El Camino Real de Tierra Adentro, the oldest continuously used European roadway in North America, the Gutiérrez-Hubbell House enjoyed a favored location.

The Gutiérrez-Hubbell House was a mercantile, trading post, stagecoach stop, and post office. Photo by Ashley M. Biggers.

GUTIÉRREZ-HUBBELL HOUSE

What: Territorial-era entrepreneurs

Where: 6029 Isleta Blvd. SW

Cost: By donation

Pro Tip: Explore the grounds and visit the New Mexico dahl sheep kept on the adjoining property. BernCo Bernie, the mascot of Bernalillo County, is one of the inhabitants.

the couple's twelve children, took after his father, becoming a merchant and trader. He established the famed Hubbell Trading Post (now a National Historic Site) in Ganado, Arizona. Louisa Hubbell was the Gutiérrez-Hubbell House's final familial inhabitant; she died in 1996. In 2007, Cornerstones, a preservation nonprofit, led a restoration of the 5,700-square-foot home. The effort preserved the home's twenty-seven-inch-thick adobe walls—a hallmark of the era's architecture—and reimagined the trading post as it once was. The home opened as a museum in 2014 and is now listed on the State Register of Cultural Properties. The ten-acre plot includes heritage apple trees from the original orchard and, perhaps, some of the first grafts of New Mexico wine grapes.

BENEATH THE SURFACE

How did a vacant Rio Grande Pueblo escape excavation?

Unremarkable hills on a sagebrush mesa on Albuquerque's west side are the only clues marking the location of Piedras Marcadas Pueblo—one of the few unexcavated pueblos in the Rio Grande Valley. Dr. Matthew Schmader, an adjunct anthropology professor at the University of New Mexico and former Albuquerque Open Space division director, has been involved in preserving and researching this significant cultural site since the 1980s.

Schmader has documented the sprawling site using equipment that emits electrical currents. Built beginning in the 1300s, it was a two- to three-story adobe village with more than one thousand rooms that may have housed several thousand people at its peak. The ancestors of today's Sandia and Isleta Puebloans had migrated to other areas by the 1620s, after the arrival of the Spanish forever changed Pueblo life.

Above ground, a pottery sherd carpet with pieces from different eras testifies to its former Pueblo residents. Below ground lies some six feet of "cultural fill"— anthropologist speak for evidence of former inhabitants— that includes Spanish musket balls and arrow heads that tell a tale of a Spanish attack on the fortress and the

---

Piedras Marcadas Pueblo is one of the few unexcavated pueblos in the Rio Grande Valley.

The grounds of Piedras Marcadas Pueblo are a carpet of pottery sherds testifying to its connection to another time. Photo by Ashley M. Biggers.

Pueblos' defense. "No matter how you slice it, this is a place of an intense standoff between the expedition and the Pueblo fighting for survival," Schmader says.

Piedras Marcadas Pueblo escaped the fate of other pueblo sites—many have been built over or excavated—through a series of historical accidents. It escaped agricultural leveling during the Spanish Colonial and homesteading periods because it was high ground. Later, it was held in private ownership until the City of Albuquerque purchased it thirty years ago.

PIEDRAS MARCADAS PUEBLO

What: Unexcavated pueblo

Where: Open Space Visitor Center, 6500 Coors Blvd. NW

Cost: None

Pro Tip: Visitation to this site is limited and is available only by guided tour. To understand the ancestral Pueblo culture that once lived here, visit Piedras Marcadas Canyon at Petroglyphs National Monument. Puebloans who held specific roles, e.g., medicine men and chiefs, traveled to the canyon to leave their marks there. For tours and information about Piedras Marcadas Pueblo, contact the Open Space Visitor Center.

OFF THE MAIN TRAIL

How can you get off the beaten path at the petroglyphs?

Petroglyphs National Monument is Albuquerque's national park. Stretching seventeen miles along the West Mesa, the monument protects some twenty-five thousand petroglyphs, which makes it one of the largest petroglyph sites in North America. Native American and Spanish settlers etched designs and symbols into the volcanic basalt escarpment here from four hundred to seven hundred years ago. The artists created petroglyphs by pecking away the varnish, or patina, on the surface of the rock to reveal the lighter rock underneath. The monument is one of the most visited attractions in the city, and 80 percent of visitors head straight to Boca Negra Canyon, probably because it's easy walking. But that trail doesn't hold a candle to other areas of the park, which is co-managed by the National Park Service and the Albuquerque Open Space Division.

Instead of following the well-traveled path of Boca Negra Canyon, head to Piedras Marcadas Canyon, where three hundred to five hundred petroglyphs unfold over a 1.5-mile loop trail—the highest concentration of petroglyphs along the park's trails. Hawks soar above the field of boulders marked with human figures and symbols,

---

The Piedras Marcadas Canyon features unique petroglyphs in which a masked face bends over the edge or around the corner of a boulder.

Piedras Marcadas Canyon has the highest concentrations of rock carvings in Petroglyph National Monument. *Photo by Ashley M. Biggers.*

PETROGLYPH NATIONAL MONUMENT

What: Many markings

Where: Piedras Marcadas Canyon is located on Golf Course Road at Jill Patricia Street. The parking lot is behind the Valvoline Motor Oil station.

Cost: None

Pro Tip: Piedras Marcadas Canyon has an undeveloped trail system. There are no water stations or restrooms available; prepare accordingly.

such as kokopelli; handprints; animals, such as gambol quail; and geometric designs. Most of the markings date to around 1300 AD, though symbols such as crosses reflect the Spanish arrival in 1540. Bullet holes testify to more recent additions. Most of the petroglyphs' meanings are known only to those who created the markings and those who shared their cultures, but observers can appreciate these expressions and their profound spiritual significance, too.

DOES NOT COMPUTE

Where is Microsoft's first office?

When people think of Microsoft's headquarters, they likely picture Seattle, Washington. However, the company that transformed the world with personal computing software got its start in Albuquerque.

In the mid-1970s, Microsoft co-founder Paul Allen was working at Honeywell, in Massachusetts, when he saw an article in *Popular Electronics* about the Altair 8800—the first microcomputer. Allen contacted his high-school friend Bill Gates, who shared Allen's fascination with the possibilities of personal computing.

Allen pitched a BASIC software program to Micro Instrumentation and Telemetry Systems, the Albuquerque company that made the Altair. The company accepted the pitch. The only problem? Allen didn't actually have a working program at the time. Nevertheless, Gates quit Harvard to join Allen in Albuquerque. They founded their company in 1975, naming it Micro Soft, a portmanteau of microcomputer and software.

Gates and Allen lived in the Sundowner Motel along Route 66, where they wrote a version of the programming

---

HISTORIC MICROSOFT HEADQUARTERS

What: Birthplace of personal computing

Where: 115 California St. NE

Cost: None

Pro Tip: When Allen returned to Albuquerque, his first stop was often his favorite restaurant, Duran Central Pharmacy. His go-to order was the green chile enchilada and a tamale with red chile, with a flour tortilla on the side.

Microsoft is most associated with Seattle, Washington, but the software giant got its start in this beige-brick office building in Albuquerque. Photo by Ashley M. Biggers.

language that would become the game-changing Microsoft software. A few blocks away, a nondescript office at 115 California Street Northeast served as their headquarters. There they pursued their vision of "a computer on every desk and in every home."

The company's time in the Duke City was short. By 1979, the company had relocated to its current home in Bellevue, Washington. However, Albuquerque remains the cradle of personal computing.

Gates ran afoul of the law twice in Albuquerque. In 1975, police arrested him for speeding and driving without a license. Then, in 1977, Gates earned his now famous mug shot for running a stop sign and driving without a license.

THE SECRET GATE

Where did KGB tradecraft take place in the Duke City?

The Spy House (see page 16) isn't the only place in Albuquerque where top-secret information passed into Soviet hands. On August 5, 1945, Theodore Hall met operative Lona Cohen, code name Leslie, at the University of New Mexico's main entrance at Central Avenue and Yale Boulevard. They wandered the campus exchanging information about Hall's work.

Hall was an eighteen-year-old physics prodigy from Harvard University when he began working on the Manhattan Project in Los Alamos, New Mexico, in January 1944. Even as a junior physicist, he analyzed whether weapons-grade plutonium could be used on a gun-type bomb design. In October, he contacted the KGB and volunteered to be a spy. He reported to the KGB that scientists in Los Alamos were working on not one but two different types of bombs. When the information rang true, the KGB accepted and issued him the code name MLLAD. He met with an operative in Albuquerque, at the intersection of First and Central, in May 1945. During the meeting he predicted that the Americans would have enough weapons-grade plutonium for one bomb by August or September 1945.

Hall, a.k.a. MLLAD, returned to the University of New Mexico in 1986 to speak at a conference; his hosts were unaware of his past.

KGB agent code name MLLAD informed his handler of the success of the Trinity Test at the University of New Mexico's main entrance on Central Avenue and Yale Boulevard. Photo by Ashley M. Biggers.

His August 1945 meeting with Leslie at the University of New Mexico was meant to provide details about the success of the Trinity Test (when the world's first atomic bomb was detonated in the desert outside Alamogordo, New Mexico). Ironically, the meeting took place just one day before the August 6 bombing of Hiroshima, Japan. By the time the Soviets received MLLAD's intel, they were already well aware that the United States had a working nuclear weapon. The Army honorably discharged Hall in 1946 without knowledge of his clandestine actions. In 1950, the Venona project, which decrypted Soviet Union intelligence agency messages, revealed Hall as a spy.

UNIVERSITY OF NEW MEXICO

What: Clandestine meeting place

Where: Central Avenue and Yale Boulevard Southeast

Cost: None

Pro Tip: While you're on campus, check out the Smith Family Totem Pole (see page 42).

THE FIRST ASCENSION

When did the first hot-air balloon fly over Albuquerque?

Albuquerque is known as the hot-air ballooning capital of the world—thanks in no small part to the Albuquerque International Balloon Fiesta, the largest ballooning event in the world. Ballooning history buffs—and longtime Albuquerqueans—will recall that the now world-famous balloon fiesta got its start with thirteen balloons in a mall parking lot on April 8, 1972.

However, Duke City ballooning history started nearly a century earlier on July 4, 1882. Albuquerque bartender Park Van Tassel—who somehow earned the nickname "Professor"—flew a coal gas–powered balloon as part of the city's Fourth of July celebrations. The balloon had a thirty-thousand-cubic-foot envelope. (Modern-day balloons are around sixty-five thousand cubic feet.) Even so, filling the balloon took hours, so long that many spectators who had initially gathered at the inflation site drifted back to Old Town for the celebrations and missed the spectacle.

> Van Tassel's feat was remarkable, so much so that he tried it again in September during the second annual New Mexico Territorial Fair. On this occasion, while he was inflating the balloon, the tethers broke, and his ride left without him.

This parking lot was once the site of Albuquerque's first hot-air balloon ascension. Photo by Nick Cessac.

FIRST BALLOON FLIGHT

What: Van Tassel's launch point

Where: Second Street between Central Avenue and Gold Street

Cost: None

Pro Tip: While you're at this intersection, walk a block north to check out a historic Hilton hotel (page 76).

Eventually, he took flight. Van Tassel is credited as being the first to discover the famous "Albuquerque Box"—albeit accidentally. These conditions help pilots fly longer over a relatively small area of the city by taking advantage of winds moving in two different directions at different altitudes. He drifted over the city for a while before his balloon, dubbed the City of Albuquerque, flew to an astonishing fourteen thousand feet. (Most hot-air balloons cruise at around 1,200 to 3,000 feet.) The pilot began throwing items overboard to hasten his descent. He was successful, but perhaps a bit too much. He met a rather rough landing in a valley cornfield.

ALBUQUERQUE'S "BEACH"

How did a former dump become fishing lakes?

In 1931, the stretch of land between the Albuquerque Country Club and the Rio Grande was a former city dump. Mayor Clyde Tingley, who served in elected office for some forty years, envisioned a new identity for this acreage. He instructed the newly formed Middle Rio Grande Conservancy District to dredge the dump and install a shallow lake. Conservationist Aldo Leopold's 1917 design for a Rio Grande Park, which included a lake, may have inspired Tingley.

Then called Conservancy Beach, its waters were large enough for the speedboat races that took place there on weekends in the 1930s. The lake's waterslides, diving platform, bathhouses, and miles of shoreline for sunbathing immediately became a draw. It was a popular outdoor swimming pool until the 1950s, when polio scares closed it to swimmers.

Decades later, the U.S. Army Corps of Engineers and the City of Albuquerque teamed to create fishing, wildlife, and model boating lakes. The last of the three lakes

---

Clyde and Carrie Tingley landed in Albuquerque when, as an engaged couple, they were traveling to Arizona in search of a cure for Carrie's tuberculosis. She had an asthma attack in the Duke City, which waylaid their plans. They never left.

Tingley Beach was the site of a city dump before it was turned into swimming lakes, and now fishing ponds. Photo by Ashley M. Biggers.

reopened in 2006. Anglers line the shores, and the Duke City Model Yacht Club operates a fleet of remote-controlled vessels on these waters. Tingley and his wife, Carrie, are memorialized in bronze statues on the western edge of Tingley Beach.

TINGLEY BEACH

What: Fishing, wildlife, and model boating lakes

Where: Paseo del Bosque Trail

Cost: None

Pro Tip: Although fishing is free, you'll need a New Mexico fishing license. When you're done fishing, hop aboard the railroad that chugs to the other three ABQ BioPark destinations (the Zoo, Aquarium, and Botanic Garden).

LET'S GET PHYSICAL

Why did the Mercury astronauts get their medical clearances in Albuquerque?

Project Mercury aimed to put the first man into Earth orbit and return him safely. The Mercury Seven were the first selected to pilot these spaceflights. Before they did, they underwent rigorous medical testing to ensure they could endure the flights' physical demands. Those tests happened in Albuquerque.

William Randolph "Randy" Lovelace II (1907–1965) spearheaded the exams. Lovelace grew up in the Duke City, graduated from Harvard Medical School in 1934, and went on to work for the Mayo Clinic in Rochester, Minnesota. After time in the Army Medical Corps Reserve, his passion for flying took him to the Aeromedical Field Laboratory at Wright Field in Dayton, Ohio, where he was on a team of researchers that developed a high-altitude oxygen mask. (Lovelace, a daredevil, tested the mask himself.) He went on to active duty with the Army Air Corps during World War II and further examined the medical problems high-altitude flying introduced—often on himself.

The sudden death of two of his sons from polio in 1946 sent the family back to his hometown. In Albuquerque, he began working with his father, who had founded Lovelace Clinic. Lovelace the younger wanted to continue his work

---

The medical guidelines Lovelace helped develop were also used for the astronauts of the Gemini and Apollo programs.

The Mercury astronauts underwent physical testing at Lovelace Clinic, now the Gibson Medical Center. Photo by Ashley M. Biggers.

with aerospace medicine and, in 1958, signed on with the newly created NASA. In 1959, the original Mercury Project astronaut candidates came to Albuquerque for a week of medical testing at the Lovelace hospital (now the Gibson Medical Center).

Lovelace believed the profile of the "perfect astronaut" fit women as well as it did men. In 1960, he chose twenty-five women to undergo testing. Putting women on the astronaut track didn't seem as out of place to Lovelace as it did to his colleagues. "He was surrounded by strong women—his wife and three daughters," his niece Mary Ann Bunten says. NASA named the selected female astronauts the Mercury Thirteen, but the program was abruptly scuttled the next year before they could take flight.

NASA eventually promoted Lovelace and named him director of space medicine. He held the position for only a year before he and his wife were killed in a plane crash in 1965, thus bringing to an end Albuquerque's astronaut testing.

> **LOVELACE CLINIC/ GIBSON MEDICAL CENTER**
>
> **What:** Former astronaut testing center
>
> **Where:** 5400 Gibson Blvd. SE
>
> **Cost:** None
>
> **Pro Tip:** This is a working medical facility, so it's best to appreciate the history from the outside.

GLASS GARDEN

Why are there acres of glittering glass in the Bosque?

A three-acre stretch of land along the Rio Grande bosque (cottonwood forest) is carpeted with blue, green, white, and brown glass shards. It's evidence of one of the city's early landfills. Residents used this dump site from 1932 to 1946, when municipal trash pick-up was instituted. The site highlights how the city's stance on the Bosque has evolved. "It's a protected area today. It's not a place we go and dump our trash," says Albuquerque Open Space Division forestry supervisor Matthew Peterson.

Because there were no plastic containers during that period—and recycling was not yet a formal practice, though reusing certainly was—the plot is littered with glass containers. Over the years, other detritus, such as newspapers, has disintegrated. The glass remains. You may spot pieces of dishware, glass containers, and even Clorox bleach bottles.

The glass has worn smooth over the years, so it's quite safe to walk on and around.

GLASS GARDEN

What: Field of millions of pieces of colored glass

Where: Albuquerque Open Space, 2315 Second St. SW

Cost: None

Pro Tip: A spray-painted sign on Second Street marks the turn west along a short road to a parking area. From the parking area, cross the multi-use path and walk up the short rise and across the drainage ditch. Follow the access road to the start of the Glass Garden. Beyond the access road, there are few paths through the area.

The ground at the Glass Garden is littered with shards of bottles and dishware. Photo by Ashley M. Biggers.

The acreage feels like an archaeological site, with relics more modern than the pottery shards New Mexicans may find elsewhere but no less emblematic of the culture. "It never made it onto the state historical preservation list," Peterson says. "But it is believed to have some historical significance."

Artists venture here to collect glass for found-art creations and have even led glass-collecting workshops at the Glass Garden. However, most prefer to let the garden, and its shiny remains, lie.

WELL, SHOOT

Why are there cannons in Old Town Plaza?

Old Town Plaza isn't just Albuquerque's founding neighborhood; it's a microcosm of Duke City history. The flags of five governing bodies have flown over the square—Spain, Mexico, the United States, New Mexico, and the Confederacy.

During the Civil War, Texas Confederates under the command of Brigadier General H. H. Sibley invaded the territory and occupied Albuquerque for about six weeks in 1862. General Sibley then headed north, leaving Major Trevanion T. Teel in charge. On April 9, Union Col. E. R. S. Canby made the first attack in the "Battle of Albuquerque." By April 12, the Confederates didn't have enough ammunition left for a fight and were subsisting on limited rations.

Teel lowered the Confederate flag so they could retreat. But first they buried eight cannons so the pursuing Union soldiers couldn't recover them. In 1889, Teel, by then an elderly man, returned and revealed the location of the buried Mountain Howitzers—in a chile field north of San Felipe de Neri Church. If he'd kept his secret, they might still be buried beneath the Albuquerque Museum (at 2000 Mountain Road Northwest) instead of displayed inside

---

The Confederate flag has flown over Old Town more recently than the Civil War. Activists campaigned and had the flag removed in 2015.

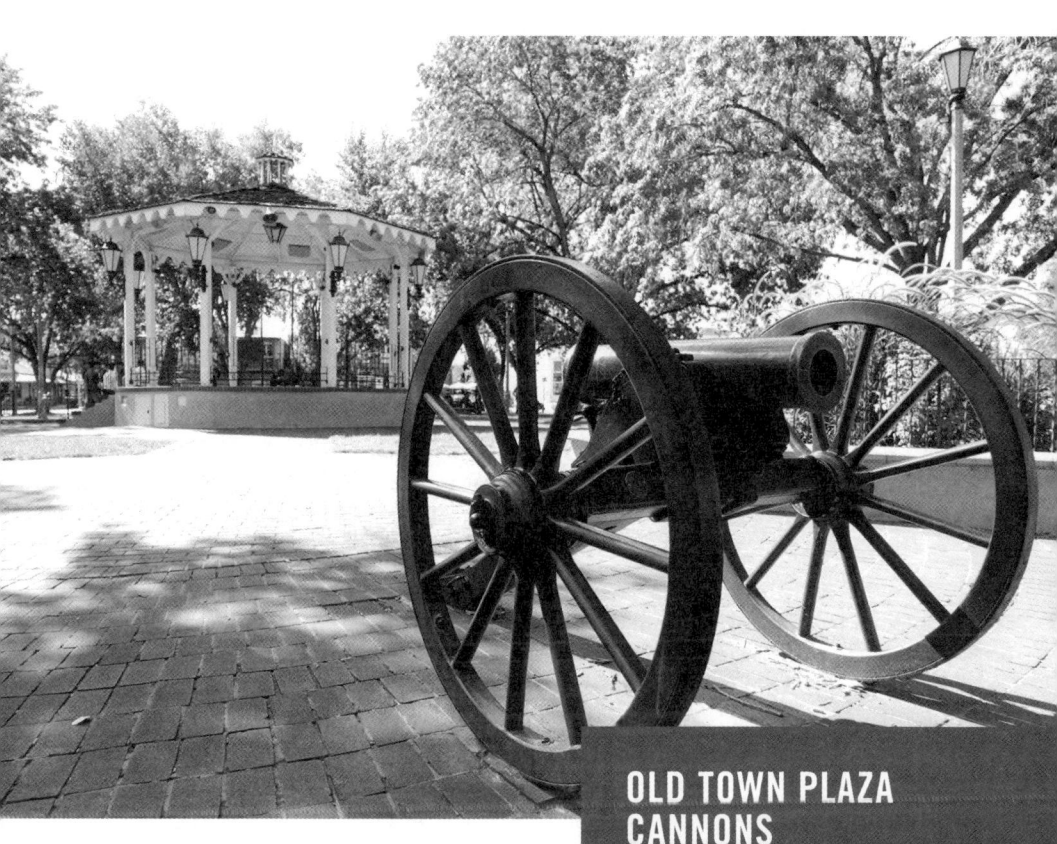

Replica mountain howitzers in Old Town Plaza are reminders of Albuquerque's Civil War past, when it was, for a time, under control of the Confederate Army. Photo by Nick Cessac.

OLD TOWN PLAZA CANNONS

What: Evidence of Albuquerque's days in the Confederacy

Where: 200 N. Plaza St. NW

Cost: None

Pro Tip: Join an Old Town tour guided by Albuquerque Museum docents Sunday, Tuesday, Thursday, and Friday, April through November.

it, where two of the originals are part of the permanent collection. Replicas are displayed on Old Town Plaza.

ARTISTIC FOSSILS

How did the Duke City hatch an Arroyosaurus?

In 1998, an arroyo (water drainage channel) project became a work of art. After the Albuquerque Metropolitan Arroyo Flood Control Authority completed its utilitarian work on the Calabacillas Arroyo, artist Michael G. Wallace cast artificial fossils in the channel walls. Kevin Troutman, AMAFCA GIS manager, says, "It was going to be in a populated area, so we thought, 'Let's make it look good.'" As the largest arroyo on the city's west side, Calabacillas Arroyo extends seventeen miles, but the fossils can be found in the portion just east of Coors Boulevard. In that section, white forms depict a variety of objects from New Mexico's history, from the Precambrian era to the future, which is represented by the footprints of a baby.

    The fossils look as though they are embedded in rock layers, with occasional strata and faults denoting eras. Forms trickle down the channel's north and south sides. The largest and most eye-catching of these (even occasionally from Coors Boulevard) is known as the "Arroyosaurus"; it looks like the skeleton of a Tyrannosaurus rex. This predator is followed by the bones of a saber-toothed cat and a mammoth. The forms become more modern as they flow east. They depict a conquistador

---

> A scavenger hunt on the AMAFCA website (amafca.org) provides visitors with a fossil checklist.

A drainage channel on Albuquerque's west side contains a fossil of a rare creature, the Arroyosaurus, along with other creatures and artifacts representing local history. Photo by Ashley M. Biggers.

THE FOSSIL PROJECT

What: Calabacillas Arroyo

Where: From Coors Boulevard (north of Paseo del Norte Boulevard), turn east along Westside Drive Northwest. Follow that road downhill; before it turns south and becomes Riverfront Road Northwest, there is a parking area to the left (north).

Cost: None

Pro Tip: Visitors are welcome along the paths on both sides of the channel and are able to cross through the channel to view the alternate side. However, keep in mind that in times of rainfall, ditches are deadly and should be avoided.

helmet (marking the arrival of the Spanish), a wagon wheel (representing the advent of the Santa Fe Trail), and the "Fat Man" atomic bomb (the arrival of the Atomic Age), to name a few. The fossils also include a Jell-O box (see the entry on the Spy House on page 16 for more on this item).

INTO THE STACKS

Why does a university museum have a totem pole?

A Tlowitsis crest pole, commonly known as a totem pole, towers in the lobby of the Maxwell Museum of Anthropology offices, to the south of the Maxwell Museum of Anthropology proper. The Tlowitsis Nation's traditional territories span the coastal area of North Vancouver Island in British Columbia. So how did one of its totem poles end up in Albuquerque?

Archaeologist Dr. Frank Hibben acquired the totem pole in 1940. By some accounts, however, he did so illegally; First Nations representatives reported it missing. At best, he acquired it surreptitiously. Hibben was a University of New Mexico professor and a long-running director of the Maxwell Museum, so the pole became part of the museum's collection.

A kingfisher, human, wolf, humpback whale, river otter, great horned owl, and first man all find places along the crest pole. Renowned Kwakwaka'wakw artist Yakuglas (or Charlie James) carved the pole in 1907. After arriving at the University of New Mexico in the 1940s, it sat outside for decades; the faded, sun-worn pole was moved inside in 2017.

That same year, a descendent of the original carvers and commissioners, Tom Hunt, Jr., with apprentice Bertram Smith, restored the pole to its former glory,

---

The Maxwell Museum of Anthropology is the city's oldest public museum.

A totem from indigenous peoples in British Columbia is a rarity in the Southwest. Photos by Ashley M. Biggers. Photos printed with the permission of Chief Danial Smith.

returning it to the striking black, white, and red used on it when commercial paints were first available.

In 2017, the university returned the pole's title to the Tlowitsis Nation, and in particular the Smith family; it is the hereditary pole of Chief Danial Smith. The university and the nation developed a thirty-year repository agreement, so the pole will remain in the museum's physical possession for the next three decades.

SMITH FAMILY TOTEM

What: Pacific Northwest totem in the Southwest

Where: Maxwell Museum of Anthropology, 500 University Blvd. NE

Cost: None, donations appreciated

Pro Tip: Founded in 1932 in conjunction with the university's prestigious anthropology department, the Maxwell Museum's collections are vast—some three million objects. They include one of the oldest and largest Navajo rug collections, four-thousand-year-old cuneiform tablets, and Hungarian swords from the Bronze Age, just to name a few.

43

FROM THE FIRE

Why is there a chainsaw sculpture garden in the Bosque?

Firefighter Mark Chavez has transformed fire-scorched acreage in the Bosque into a destination. In 2003, teenagers sparked a fire in the riverside cottonwood forests while playing with fireworks. The blaze roared through the forest, burning between 100 and 250 acres along the Rio Grande.

Chavez helped fight the fire, then turned to his hobby to leave another lasting mark on this place. He's a self-taught chainsaw sculpture artist, so he set to work turning ten dead trees into rough-hewn sculptures dedicated to local wildlife, Southwest culture, and the firefighters. Sculptures in the garden depict a bald eagle rising from flames; coyotes howling; and heron, squirrels, and turtles.

Two sculptures have symbolic significance. One depicts La Llorona, a famous figure in Latin American and New Mexican folklore who wanders the river calling out for her dead children—and snatching children wandering alone. Another sculpture pays homage to firefighters with the proud figure of a fireman standing on a defeated dragon, representing those who conquered the blaze here.

Chavez is now retired from firefighting and works exclusively on his art through Sandia Bear Company.

Firefighter Mark Chavez used a chainsaw to carve the figures like this bald eagle that make up the Pueblo Montaño Chainsaw Sculpture Garden. Photo by Ashley M. Biggers.

PUEBLO MONTAÑO CHAINSAW SCULPTURE GARDEN

What: Bosque burn scar turned sculpture garden

Where: Pueblo Montaño Picnic Area and Trailhead, 4100-4112 Montaño Rd. NW

Cost: None

Pro Tip: The chainsaw garden provides access to trails through the Bosque, including the sixteen-mile Paseo del Bosque Trail.

In firefighter lore, a dragon is an uncontrollable blaze. Artist Mark Chavez carved a firefighter conquering the blaze. Photo by Ashley M. Biggers.

THORNY FROSTY

Who builds Albuquerque's tumbleweed snowman?

Albuquerqueans are nothing if not resourceful. In 1995, the Albuquerque Metropolitan Arroyo Flood Control Authority started building a snowman with one of the city's most ample resources: tumbleweeds. What started out as a bit of good fun has become a serious endeavor as AMAFCA upholds one of the city's most treasured holiday traditions.

Each year the AMAFCA Tumbleweed Snowman has grown. He started out just a couple of feet tall; now he averages twelve feet tall. Since he blew away in a windstorm in 2011, AMAFCA crews have taken measures to secure their stout snowman. They construct a support structure with an eight-foot-diameter base and a two-inch rebar pole in the middle to ensure the tumbleweeds stay put.

AMAFCA's welder, James Moya, and two other maintenance crew members assemble the snowman the Tuesday after Thanksgiving (a.k.a. Tumbleweed Tuesday). The snowman is taken down each January 2.

Crew members hunt down the materials a few days before Thanksgiving. The tumbleweed snowman is decked out using recycled materials. He dons a jaunty

---

TUMBLEWEED SNOWMAN

What: A snowman fit for the desert

Where: AMAFCA offices, 2600 Prospect Ave. NE

Cost: None

Pro Tip: The snowman is constructed behind the AMAFCA offices but is visible from westbound I-40, just before exit 159D.

The Tumbleweed Snowman is an Albuquerque tradition. Photo courtesy of AMAFCA.

fifty-five-gallon drum for a hat. His hands are old work gloves—oddly, he usually has two left hands. A broken ax handle makes his nose, and scrap metal disks and rebar make his eyes, buttons, and mouth. He has one fresh accessory though: every year Moya's mother knits him a new scarf.

AMAFCA hasn't had to grow its own tumbleweeds for the snowman yet, but they considered it during a 2017 drought that made materials scarce.

ROLLING ALONG

Where does the last duty board in Rail Yards history still hang?

The duty board from January 20, 1977—the last ever used in the Albuquerque Rail Yards—hangs in the Wheels Museum. The board, which outlines each worker's responsibilities for that day, marks the end of a period of history that molded the Duke City into, well, a city at all.

The Atlantic and Pacific Railroad began establishing what is now known as the Rail Yards in 1880. The railroad could have easily chosen Belen or Bernalillo for its back shops, where it repaired cars, but land values priced them out of those towns. The railroad also considered locating the facility in Old Town, but the residents protested the railroad's arrival. Instead, the railroad chose a site on higher ground, near what is now Second Street and Atlantic Avenue. Even there, the back shops experienced flooding. Leba Freed, executive director of the Wheels Museum, says there are two railcars buried on site to act as ballasts. The shops made Albuquerque the home of the largest repair facility between Chicago and Los Angeles. By the 1920s, the repair facility employed around a thousand workers—a substantial number considering a 1910 census recorded the population of Albuquerque as thirteen thousand.

The storehouse building once stocked some thirty thousand parts used in locomotive repairs.

The Wheels Museum celebrates everything on wheels. Photo by Ashley M. Biggers.

Most of the buildings on site were built between 1914 and 1924. That includes the blacksmith shop, the site of today's Rail Yards Market; a firehouse, which was Albuquerque's first fire station; and a storehouse. Today, the latter building houses the off-the-beaten-path Wheels Museum devoted to all things on wheels. The museum opened in 2008, shortly after the City of Albuquerque saved the Rail Yards from being razed for development in 2007.

The duty board is just one of the historical treasures in its sprawling collection. There's a vast assemblage of original artifacts from the Alvarado Hotel—Albuquerque's Fred Harvey hotel that was torn down in 1970. These items include an original Harvey Girl uniform, a headboard, a copper ice-cream mold, and even a bathmat embossed with the Fred Harvey name. Elsewhere in the collections, you'll find a safe used aboard the Santa Fe Railroad until 2008 sitting side by side with a horse-drawn Bezemek Dairy wagon from Corrales.

WHEELS MUSEUM

What: Railroad artifacts

Where: 1100 Second St. SW

Cost: By donation

Pro Tip: Ask to see the transfer station in back—it's the last remaining of its kind in the United States.

NAH, I'M GONNA STAY AT THE DISCO

How can you do silent disco yoga?

Silent discos are a far cry from the discos of the seventies. Instead of "Stayin' Alive" or "Dancing Queen" blaring over speakers, those same tunes—or modern-day hits—play through headsets. Silent discos are common in big cities and at music festivals across the United States.

Mobile studio YogaZo founder Ashley Fathergill first attended a silent disco at a music festival out of state, then gave the technology a yogic bend by bringing it to her students' practices. She is the only teacher in New Mexico offering the practice outside the festival environment. Her YogaZo mobile studio hopscotches across the city with pop-up classes at the city's museums, on rooftops, and in breweries—all with the goal of creating a place where everyone is welcome on their mat. YogaZo offers silent disco yoga four to five times a year at similarly varied locations.

With the headsets on, students hear only the sounds of the instructor and the music. It hones and deepens their practices without the distraction of hearing other students move around them. Fathergill invites students to close

---

YogaZo donates a portion of its proceeds to local nonprofits, including Animal Humane New Mexico.

Ashley Fathergill, founder of Yoga Zo, teaches a pop-up silent disco yoga class in the Rail Yards. Photo by Brandon Barela, courtesy of YogaZo.

their eyes, further isolating the senses. In Fathergill's hands, the music playlists at the silent disco may be nineties hits or rock anthems, but it's always a one-of-a-kind experience.

YOGAZO STUDIO

What: Silent disco yoga

Where: See yogazoabq.com for dates and locations.

Cost: Varies

Pro Tip: YogaZo classes are approachable for all levels of yogis—even those who have never taken a class before.

CARD READER

How can you get your fortune told by a goose?

Princess Esmeralda is a fixture at the Downtown Growers Market. She reads Osho Zen tarot cards and speaks with her handler, Anand Naren, better known as Oma, to share what she sees. "I speak goose talk," Oma says. Then, leaning close, he adds, "It's a little bit of BS. But it's the kind of BS that makes people smile."

Princess Esmeralda and Oma, with his flowing robes, long beard, and rope sandals, have been reading cards together for five years. "Geese have a reputation for being foolish. But they're not foolish. They are quite wise, sensitive, and wonderful creatures. Who can resist a goose?" he asks. Not many people. The unusual sight of a fortune-telling goose brings curious passersby over for readings. They cautiously select a card and are usually delighted with Oma's wise, gentle nature and his knack for delivering a message they need to hear. He says the cards relay messages for discovery and breakthrough. He tells stories through the cards to help people "know who they are. I hope people go away feeling a little better."

In addition to reading cards, Oma is a clay artist who sells his work at the market stand. His sculpted goddesses, angels, and dainty clay birds fit in the palm of your hand. "Birds are my favorite people," he says.

On his days off, Oma is a whirling dervish—an order of Sufis who meditate through spinning.

Oma and Princess Esmeralda share their tarot wisdom at the Downtown Growers Market. Photo by Ashley M. Biggers.

PRINCESS ESMERALDA AND OMA

What: Fortune-telling goose

Where: Downtown Growers Market, Robinson Park, 810 Copper Ave. NW

Cost: By donation

Pro Tip: The Downtown Growers Market season runs early April to late October on Saturday mornings.

GOTCHA DAY

What are adopted signs?

Cruising Route 66 isn't as glorious as it was in the Mother Road's heyday; today, many of the signs along the route are derelict, calling attention to long-shuttered businesses in faded, chipped paint. The nonprofit Friends of the Orphan Signs adopts these empty signs, called "orphans" in the historic preservation community. The group then brings together professional and amateur artists to transform the signs from tumble-down to triumphant.

Since it incorporated in 2010, the group has refurbished (not restored) a handful of signs across the city thanks to National Endowment for the Arts, City of Albuquerque public art, and other foundation funding. Some installations are permanent, as is the case with the sign at Casa Barelas (formerly the Filling Station). Members of the Barelas neighborhood and artists collaborated on the sign's design in the historic district.

At Harwood Art Center, artists Lindsey Fromm and Myriam Tapp led youth and parents from the Escuela del Sol Montessori through a weekend workshop that resulted in the permanent installation at Sixth Street and Mountain Road called the Seedling Sign. The sign features patterns

---

Friends of the Orphan Signs circumvents traditional art spaces. Its signs are immediately accessible to the public and can be widely seen—if you take the time to notice them.

The Friends of the Orphan Signs adopt derelict signs across Albuquerque. These got extra artistic help from students at the Media Arts Collaborative Charter School. Photos by Nick Cessac.

ORPHAN SIGNS

What: Adopted vintage signs

Where: 4401 Central Ave. NE (Media Arts Collaborative Charter School)

Cost: None

Pro Tip: Look for an adopted sign underway at the former Sundowner Motel at 6101 Central Avenue Northeast. For other locations visit friendsoftheorphansigns.org.

on one side and drawings of an owl and anthropomorphized animals on the other.

    Other projects are ephemeral. The students of the Media Arts Collaborative Charter School have adopted several signs in front of their school campus; thus, the creations change each semester.

WITH THANKS

Why is New Mexico the only state to have two French 40 & 8 boxcars?

New Mexico is home to not one but two boxcars from the Gratitude Train. This historic gift from France actually began with the United States extending aid. In 1947, journalist Drew Pearson spearheaded an effort to collect food, clothing, and necessities to send to war-ravaged France. The project earned the name the Friendship Train.

A few years later, Andre Picard, a French railroad worker and war veteran, organized the Gratitude Train. The project gathered thank-you gifts to send to Americans in 40 & 8 boxcars. One boxcar went to each of the forty-eight states and Washington, DC. New Mexico's boxcar arrived in Santa Fe in February 1949 to great fanfare. The gifts were distributed to libraries, museums, and colleges around the state.

Eventually the boxcar made its way to Expo New Mexico (the New Mexico State Fairgrounds), where it sat in the sun and weather for years. A member of the 40 & 8 Society discovered it in a state of disrepair in 1981. The French Boxcar Committee (composed of members from the Historical Society of New Mexico, l'Alliance Française

> **THE GRATITUDE TRAIN BOXCARS**
>
> **What:** Historic French 40 & 8 boxcars
>
> **Where:** Expo New Mexico, 300 San Pedro Dr. NE
>
> **Cost:** Varies, during the New Mexico State Fair from $10 plus parking
>
> **Pro Tip:** The boxcars are housed under a pavilion near the gate off of San Pedro Drive.

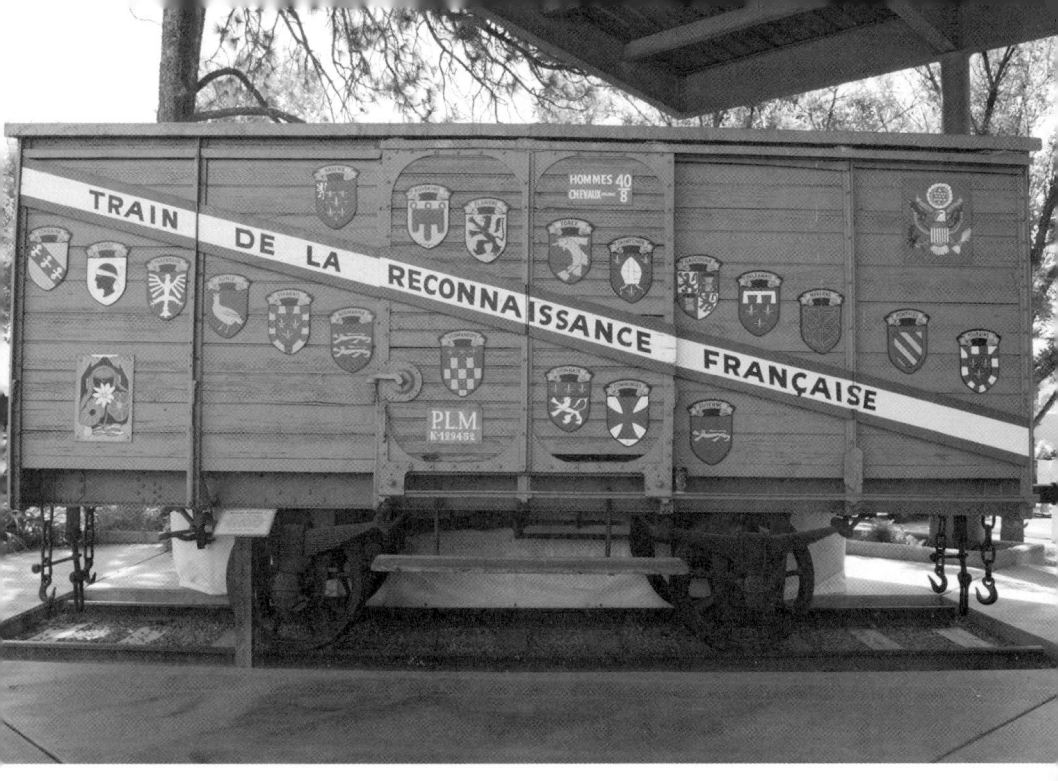

Expo New Mexico displays both New Mexico's original 40 & 8 boxcar from the 1949 Gratitude Train and a rebuilt car. Photo by Ashley M. Biggers.

d'Albuquerque, the Railroad Club of New Mexico, and the 40 & 8 Society) organized and, in 1986, purchased an antique 1903 boxcar similar to the one from the original Gratitude Train. The committee members renovated and decorated it to look just as the authentic boxcar did when it arrived in Santa Fe in 1949. New Mexico became the only state in the United States to have two of these boxcars. Expo New Mexico displays both the original and the look-alike—under a shelter.

Boxcar #2 bears the emblems of the thirteen French provinces.

FAMILY FARMERS

Where can you pick your own green chile?

In Albuquerque, many residents look forward to chile season as though it were a national holiday. When it hits, there's a scramble to buy fresh green chile; roast it; and peel, seed, and freeze it to make it last. There are numerous places to buy green chile—but only one where chile fiends can pick their own: Big Jim Farms.

The nine-acre farm in Los Ranchos de Albuquerque may have opened only in 2016, but the family that owns it has deep agricultural roots in New Mexico. The Wagner family is now in its fourth generation of farmers. Farm namesake Jim Wagner has been farming for more than forty years on family acreage across the state, including at Wagner's Farmland Experience.

The family opened the U-PICK field so they could grow organically and welcome the community. "We wanted people to be able to know where their food comes from," says Jim's daughter Chantelle Wagner. Visitors grab baskets at the farm stand and then pick among the rows, which are separated by mild, medium, hot, and extra hot. With their baskets full, they can get their green chile roasted on site to take home.

Wagner's Farmland Experience, in Corrales, offers a corn maze and pumpkin patch.

U-PICK GREEN CHILE

What: Big Jim Farms

Where: 4474 Rio Grande Blvd. NW, Los Ranchos de Albuquerque

Cost: Admission is free. Chile is sold by the half bushel.

Pro Tip: In previous years, Big Jim Farms has opened every weekend during September and October for U-PICK. Check online (bigjimfarms.com) or call (505-459-0719) prior to your visit to confirm the hours for the current season.

The Wagner family has been farming in New Mexico for four generations. Big Jim Farms welcomes the public to pick their own green chile. Photos by Ashley M. Biggers.

FLYING HIGH

Where can you see a record-setting balloon gondola?

At the Anderson Abruzzo International Balloon Museum, a seven-foot-by-five-foot-square gondola hangs in the grand windows facing Balloon Fiesta Park. Despite being New Mexico–flag yellow, the pint-sized gondola is easy to miss. But this Kevlar and carbon fiber vessel is one of the most important in ballooning history.

In 2015, using this gondola, Albuquerque-based pilot Troy Bradley and Russian pilot Leonid Tiukhtyaev set both the distance and duration records for crossing the Pacific Ocean in a gas-filled balloon. The previous records had held for thirty years. Composite Tooling, located in Albuquerque, built the custom gondola that helped them accomplish the flight. It has a small dome in the center that enabled the pilots to take turns standing during their 160-hour, thirty-seven-minute flight. They flew 6,646 miles from Saga, Japan, to four miles off the coast of the Baja Peninsula, Mexico. (They planned for a beach landing, but a strong wind pushed them parallel to the coast instead of perpendicular to it.)

Also at the museum, check out the other gondolas on the floor beneath the *Two Eagles*. They are the original *Double Eagle V* and a replica *Double Eagle II*. The former was the first balloon to make a successful Pacific crossing;

The Anderson Abruzzo International Balloon Museum served as Mission Control for the record *Two Eagles* flight.

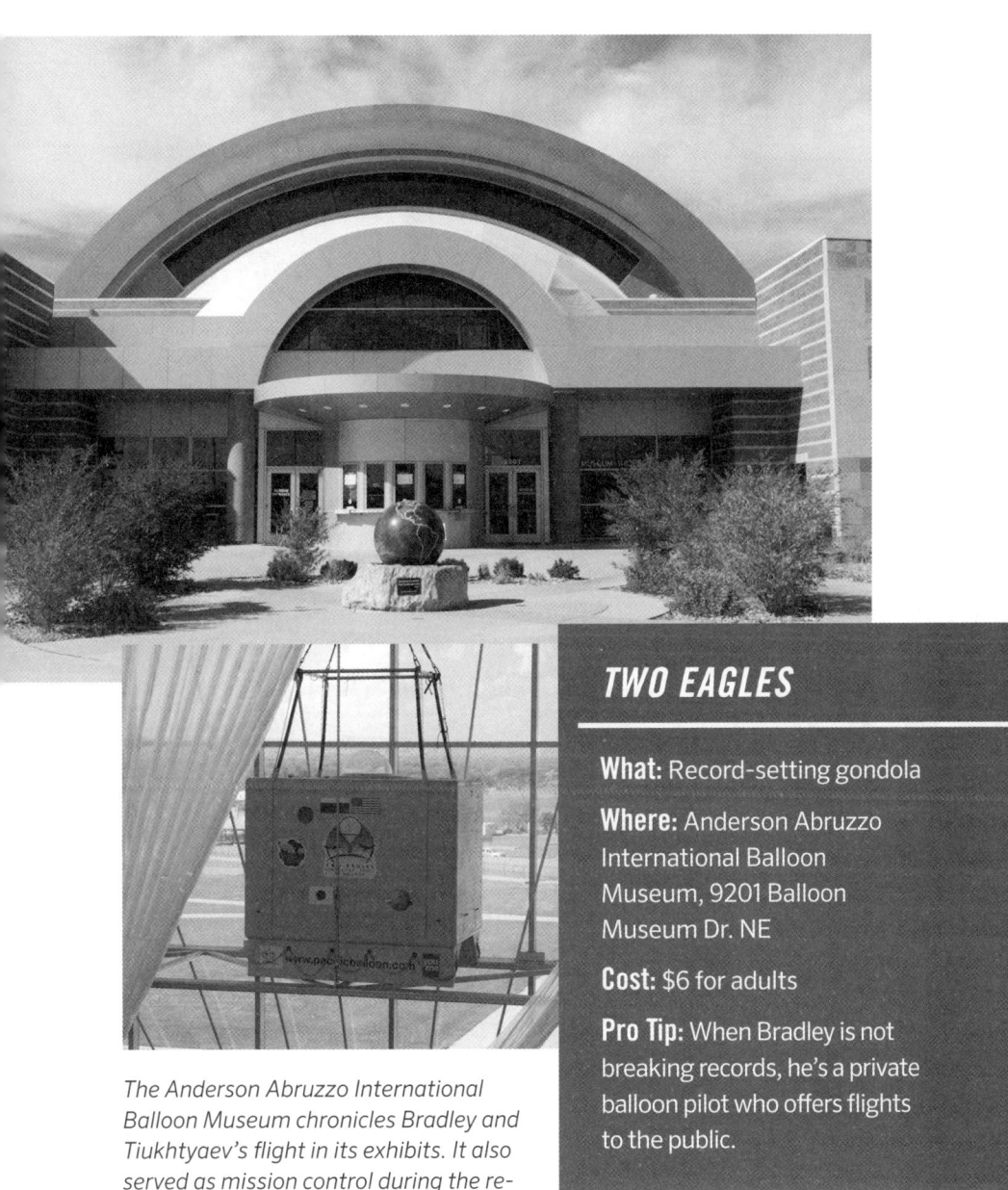

The Anderson Abruzzo International Balloon Museum chronicles Bradley and Tiukhtyaev's flight in its exhibits. It also served as mission control during the record flight. Photo by Ashley M. Biggers.

TWO EAGLES

What: Record-setting gondola

Where: Anderson Abruzzo International Balloon Museum, 9201 Balloon Museum Dr. NE

Cost: $6 for adults

Pro Tip: When Bradley is not breaking records, he's a private balloon pilot who offers flights to the public.

the latter was the first to cross the Atlantic. *Two Eagles* broke these balloons' distance and time-aloft records. Both of the balloons were also flown by Albuquerque-based pilots.

LAYER BY LAYER

Why is there a true fresco in the convention center?

Santa Fe artist Frederico Vigil has painted buon frescoes across New Mexico; California; in Alburquerque, Spain; and, yes, in the Duke City. He's one of only a handful of master fresco artists in the Southwest who specialize in true fresco—a laborious but time-tested technique that requires applying five layers of plaster. Vigil paints the final layer, with the image, as it dries.

Vigil hails from humble beginnings. His father was a barber who encouraged him and his four brothers to learn carpentry and masonry. Although Vigil's path took an artistic turn, he says he was drawn to the art because it is manual and tactile.

In November 2017, the master began a new work in a very public space: the Albuquerque Convention Center. The fresco depicts the agricultural and vinicultural history of the Rio Grande Valley. In the sketched mural, the Sandia Mountains hug one wall. On others, farmers carry baskets of grapes on their heads or stomp them in barrels. It's a four-year

---

TRUE FRESCO

What: Frederico Vigil's work in progress

Where: Albuquerque Convention Center, 401 Second St. NW

Cost: None

Pro Tip: Vigil also painted *Mundos de Mestizaje*, a monumental fresco depicting thousands of years of Hispanic history at the Torreón on the campus of the National Hispanic Cultural Center. This fresco is open to the public only during limited hours.

Artist Frederico Vigil is at work on his massive true fresco depicting the agricultural history of the Rio Grande Valley. Planning drawings and wall sketches are visible as the fresco takes shape. Photos by Ashley M. Biggers.

process to create the fresco, so until 2021 visitors can see Vigil creating his latest fresco of Albuquerque's history.

Vigil's monumental 2,500-plus-square-foot fresco at the Albuquerque Convention Center wraps around a curved stairwell between the west and east complexes, just before the Second Street sky bridge.

SUN POWERED

What's the story behind a headline-grabbing solar building?

The Solar Building was the first active solar-heated commercial building in the world. It is the site of a remarkable mechanical feat and was, at one time, world famous. Today, it is unoccupied and largely incognito. Its famous solar panels have been covered in green sheet metal.

Albuquerque architectural firm Stanley & Wright, a mid-century firm specializing in commercial and public projects, designed the building in 1956 as the offices of Bridgers & Paxton, an engineering firm. This engineering firm built the solar heating system that made the building newsworthy. The heating system had three components: collector panels, a water storage tank, and a water-to-water heat pump. The collector panels made up the building's entire south wall, which cut through the building's center at a thirty-degree angle. In total, the building had 750 square feet of solar panels. The building was heated by passing water-filled tubes through the panels. The sun warmed the water, thus warming the building. Excess heated water was stored in an underground storage tank for days without sufficient sun to heat the building. The heat pump activated if the temperature of the storage tank dropped

---

Life magazine described the solar building as "an odd-looking new office building."

Today, the Solar Building's panels have been covered with green metal roofing. Photo by Ashley M. Biggers.

beneath the temperature necessary to heat the building.

Life magazine published an article about the building, which legitimized the structure's status as a symbol of innovation in the post-war society. A few years later, in 1962, the firm added an addition to the building, and the solar system went offline. Nevertheless, the building earned a spot on the New Mexico State Register of Cultural Properties in 1985.

THE SOLAR BUILDING

What: World's first active solar-heated commercial building

Where: 213 Truman St. NE

Cost: None

Pro Tip: To learn more about buildings like this one, check out Modern Albuquerque, the guide to the Duke City's modernist architecture and mid-century history.

TORPEDO TRIBUTES

Why does a city park have submarine torpedoes in it?

Three (inert) missiles from World War II mark the entrance to USS Bullhead Memorial Park. They're part of a veterans' memorial to the fallen soldiers of the park's namesake vessel. But why does landlocked Albuquerque have a park dedicated to a submarine?

During the 1980s, the United States Submarine Veterans organization assigned every vessel to a state so its citizens could commemorate the submarines and the crewmembers who served aboard them. In either a twist of irony or a fateful selection process, they assigned New Mexico the USS *Bullhead*.

The USS *Bullhead* and eighty-four of its crewmembers met their watery ends at the hands of a Japanese bomber while patrolling the waters of Indonesia. The event occurred on August 6, 1945—the same day a nuclear weapon was dropped on Hiroshima, Japan. Of course, New Mexico and Albuquerque's Kirtland Air Force Base played a vital role in the atomic bomb's development. The first use of a nuclear weapon in war overshadowed the USS *Bullhead* tragedy. However, the

USS BULLHEAD MEMORIAL PARK

What: Veterans' memorial with torpedoes

Where: 1606 San Pedro Dr. SE

Cost: None

Pro Tip: The forty-four-acre park displays the names of the fallen crewmen on a plaque near the torpedoes.

World War II–era torpedoes make up the veterans' memorial at USS Bullhead Memorial Park. Photo by Ashley M. Biggers.

City of Albuquerque commemorates it today. The park sits along the border of Kirtland Air Force Base and adjacent to the Veterans Affairs Medical Center.

> The USS *Bullhead* was the last U.S. submarine sunk during World War II.

NO LONGER STARVING ARTISTS

Where can you see art in a former tortilla factory?

There are more artists in Albuquerque than you can fling a tortilla at. This is especially true at Sanitary Tortilla Factory, a former tortilla factory and restaurant that got a second wind as an artist studio space and gallery.

Founded by Mary and Jesse DeSoto, the first Sanitary Tortilla Factory operated off Broadway. The family brought in the city's first tortilla-making machine, which was thought to be more sanitary than making the New Mexican staple by hand. The M&J Sanitary Tortilla Factory was born. Bea and Jake Montoya bought the restaurant and tortilla factory in 1974 and moved it to the building's current location. After an unexpected rent increase, the restaurant closed in 2004. During its heyday, it was known for fresh tortillas that rolled off the conveyer belt in the back, as well as blue corn tacos, tamales, and chile rellenos. Over the years, its food was featured in the pages of the *New York Times*, the *New Yorker*, and *Cosmopolitan*. The restaurant's patrons included Barbra Streisand, Erik Estrada, and former president Bill Clinton, the latter of whom received a catered meal aboard Air Force One.

Orange tiles in the artist space pay homage to no-longer-there walls from the M&J Sanitary Tortilla Factory.

Artist Pastel painted the botanical mural on the building's exterior in 2017. Photo by Nick Cessac.

SANITARY TORTILLA FACTORY

What: Artist space in a former tortilla factory

Where: 401 Second St. SW

Cost: None

Pro Tip: Stop by the gallery during the city's Albuquerque Arts Crawl, held the first Friday of every month, when it's likely that a new exhibition is opening or an artist talk is taking place. Otherwise, the space is open by appointment only.

After M&J shuttered, Los Chileros food manufacturing company used the space until about 2012, after which time it stood vacant. Local mixed-media and installation artist sheri crider purchased the property in 2015. She writes that the space was formerly one that "historically fed [artists] and showed artists' work." It's fitting, then, that crider transformed it into fifteen below-market-value artist studios, with shared fabrication and exhibition space. "STF is honored to carry on the tradition of the beloved restaurant for more than thirty years, feeding and supporting the community through programming and exhibitions of local artists," she writes.

BLUE PLATE SPECIAL

How did a restaurant start its massive autographed plate collection?

The Range Café has quietly amassed a collection of plates that you really don't want to wash. The local restaurant chain started the tradition a bit by accident, says CEO Matt DiGregory. His business partner was a former member of the Last Mile Ramblers, a popular Western swing band in the state in the 1970s. Band member Junior Brown stopped in for a meal at the Range, and a member of the restaurant staff wanted to get his autograph. "I had seen in a restaurant once where famous people had signed [the] wall. I figured that since walls eventually had to be painted that something more tangible was in order, and that is where the plate thing started," DiGregory says.

The restaurant grew in popularity and began attracting celebrities who were in town filming movies and TV shows. Numerous stars have signed the restaurant's colorful Fiestaware-style plates, including Joe Pesci, Ed Harris, Parker Posey, Hilary Swank, Diane Keaton, and local favorite (thanks to his role in *Breaking Bad*) Bryan Cranston. Former presidents Bill Clinton and Barack Obama have both signed plates. Then there are the celebrities who've shared their autographs because of local connections. For example, *Saturday Night Live* alum Ana Gasteyer's parents live in Corrales. She's brought several

---

Cameron Diaz is the only celebrity ever to have refused to sign a plate at the Range Café.

Ted Danson is one of many actors who have signed plates. Photo by Ashley M. Biggers.

cast members in, according to DiGregory, including Will Ferrell, Lorne Michaels, Kristen Wiig, and Will Forte. Navajo code talkers from World War II have signed plates, as did hero dog Uno, a Ground Zero search-and-rescue dog from the September 11, 2001, attacks. Local actors, news anchors, and sports stars have also signed dishes.

> **RANGE CAFÉ**
>
> **What:** Autographed plate collection
>
> **Where:** 925 Camino Del Pueblo, Bernalillo
>
> **Cost:** None
>
> **Pro Tip:** While you're at the Range Café perusing plates, don't miss the dessert case.

Two plates you'll no longer see on the wall: those signed by actor/director Ron Howard and Chris Martin, lead singer of Coldplay. Both were broken when a customer fell against the wall. The latter signed a plate before he was really famous. The plate read "Nobody knows us here." A few months later, the band's single "Yellow" became a hit and everyone knew Martin.

The restaurant has more than two hundred plates in its collection. Most are at the Bernalillo location, though they're sprinkled throughout the restaurant's seven Albuquerque-area locations.

ANTHROPOLOGICAL HIJINKS

How did a cave become a scandal?

Perched high on a cliff above Las Huertas Canyon in the Sandia Mountains, a cave led to evidence that the earliest inhabitants in North America lived here thousands of years before archaeologists previously thought—at least that's what archaeologist Dr. Frank Hibben claimed when he excavated the cave in the 1930s.

As he dug through the cave's strata, he found evidence of the previously recorded Folsom culture, a Paleo-Indian culture that lived in what is now the Southwest United States ten thousand years ago. At the time, archaeologists believed them to be the Americas' earliest inhabitants. Beneath that layer, however, he found something that turned archaeologists' heads: evidence of a chipped stone spear head and animal bones. Dubbing this group of people "Sandia Man," he estimated these big-game hunters lived in the Southwest approximately twenty-five thousand years ago. When *Time* magazine reported the discovery in its May 1940 issue, the coverage cemented the discovery—and Hibben himself—as revolutionary.

However, as other archaeologists sought to substantiate his claim, they found inconsistencies in the

---

The Sandia Man Cave has been relegated to "the status of a curious old site with little value for modern investigators," according to an article in *American Antiquity*.

The entrance to the Sandia Man Cave is perched high on a wall in Las Huertas Canyon. Photo by Ashley M. Biggers.

SANDIA MAN CAVE

What: Controversial caverns

Where: The Sandia Man Cave is located on the north end of the Sandia Mountains off N.M. 165. The parking area is marked with a sign. It is a .47-mile hike from the parking area to the staircase.

Cost: None

Pro Tip: Crazy about caves? The Sandia Grotto caving club is dedicated to the exploration, conservation, and protection of caves. The group meets monthly.

samples. Disturbingly, some suggested that Hibben had planted the unique flint in the cave. Hibben seemed to skirt the controversy. He continued teaching at the University of New Mexico and overseeing the Maxwell Museum of Anthropology until his 1975 retirement. However, in 1995, journalist Douglas Preston, who is a Santa Fe resident and famous author of fiction and nonfiction, published a damning account of Hibben's research in the *New Yorker*, which led to researchers largely erasing the discovery from archaeological textbooks.

Reaching the cave itself involves a bit of a high-wire act: A circular staircase overhanging the canyon leads to a three-sided cage built around the cavern's entrance. While the public is welcome to visit the cave, venturing far beyond the entrance is discouraged.

STILL STANDING

Where does a historic Indian School still stand?

Established with the philosophy of "Kill the Indian to Save the Man," Indian Schools across the United States forcibly removed Native American children from their homes and assimilated them into Anglo culture. The Presbyterian Church founded Albuquerque Indian School in 1881. The school moved to its permanent home at Twelfth Street and Indian School in 1886. At its height in the 1960s, some twelve hundred students attended the school, according to Albuquerque Historical Society member Joe Sabatini. While other schools carted students far from home, the Albuquerque Indian School taught students from Pueblo, Diné, and Apache groups in the New Mexico area; Native American leaders had closer oversight of this school than others in the system.

One building remains from the campus: the Employees' Dormitory and Club. The building is cast in the California Mission Revival Style and is one of the city's only remaining buildings of its style. Joe Padilla (Isleta Pueblo), then the head of Albuquerque Indian School's carpentry division, and his students

INDIAN SCHOOL DORMITORY AND CLUB

What: Last remaining building of the Albuquerque Indian School

Where: 1000 Indian School Rd. NW

Cost: None

Pro Tip: The Indian Pueblo Cultural Center also sits on the former Albuquerque Indian School grounds. It's an extraordinary place to learn about the cultures of the state's nineteen Pueblo communities.

The Indian School Dormitory and Club is the last remaining building of the Albuquerque Indian School. It now houses the Native American Community Academy. Photo by Ashley M. Biggers.

designed the building. Having a Native American architect design a building is a singular achievement in Indian Boarding School history. The 1931 building served as apartments for married and single faculty members, and its dining room was used for social gatherings such as graduations and proms.

It survived the fate of other Indian School buildings because it served as the offices of the Southern Pueblos Agency. Today it houses the Native American Community Academy, a public charter school for middle and high schoolers. In addition to the core curriculum, students may take classes in Native American cultures and languages—a historical turn because the original Indian Schools aimed to eradicate all vestiges of those cultures.

The Indian School Dormitory and Club was placed on New Mexico's State Register of Cultural Properties in 1981 and the National Register of Historic Places a year later.

BEFORE THE BRAND

Where is Conrad Hilton's first high-rise hotel?

Before Conrad Hilton was the founder of one of the world's largest hotel chains, he was the son of a general store owner in San Antonio, New Mexico. He helped his father turn the general store into accommodations for traveling salesmen, a forerunner to his hotel empire. He took over the family business at age twenty-one. After stints in the New Mexico State Legislature and the U.S. Army during World War I, he moved to Texas to seek his fortune in hospitality.

In 1939, he opened his first New Mexico hotel and the first high-rise in his growing chain. The ten-story downtown Albuquerque hotel was the tallest building in the state at the time, and perhaps more importantly for the guests, it was also the state's first air-conditioned building. The hotel has welcomed several famous guests over the years, including Soviet spy Harry Gold (see page 16 for more). Manhattan Project scientists waited at the hotel on July 16, 1945, for word of the results of the Trinity Test (the world's first atomic bomb explosion). In 1946, Hilton formed the Hilton Hotels Corporation, which expanded his operations outside the United States and set the stage for his empire.

In 1969, the Hilton Hotels Corporation sold the Albuquerque hotel, which was renamed Hotel Plaza. It

---

Hilton spent his 1942 honeymoon here with his second wife, Zsa Zsa Gabor.

Conrad Hilton built his fourth hotel and first high-rise in Albuquerque. The restored building is now Hotel Andaluz Albuquerque, Curio Collection by Hilton. Photo by Nick Cessac.

HOTEL ANDALUZ ALBUQUERQUE, CURIO COLLECTION BY HILTON

What: Conrad Hilton's first high-rise hotel

Where: 125 Second St. NW

Cost: On a budget? Head to Ibiza Urban Rooftop Lounge for a drink or MÁS Tapas y Vino for small plates. Stay the night from $150.

Pro Tip: Albuquerque mayor and New Mexico governor Clyde Tingley (1881–1960) held court at the Hilton; he claimed to run the city from his favorite chair. Visitors can sit in "The Decision Chair," which is positioned by the elevators.

had several names and owners over the years. In 2005, Albuquerque businessman Gary Goodman purchased the building; it reopened three years later as the Hotel Andaluz. The name, which is short for Andalusian, evokes the Spanish region that inspired the hotel's interior design. In 2019, the hotel returned to its roots when it joined the Curio Collection by Hilton, a line of unique Hilton hotels across the globe.

MOTOR LODGE MURAL

How can you see a mural of a sacred Zuni Pueblo ceremony?

For more than a decade, the Tony Edaakie murals in De Anza Motor Lodge's basement were urban legend. They were there once—were they still? And if they had survived, could anyone see them? The historic motor lodge's redevelopment has answered these questions. The murals are there. And, yes, the public can once again see them, albeit via specific conditions aimed at respecting the murals and the cultural ceremony they depict.

Zuni art was integral to the De Anza Motor Lodge from the start. Zuni trader C. G. Wallace and his colleague S. D. Hambaugh built the motor lodge in 1939. With its admirable location along Route 66, the owners hoped to attract road-trippers with both accommodations and shopping at the in-house trading post. Wallace soon became the De Anza's sole proprietor. As tourism grew, he expanded the quintessential tourist court from thirty to sixty-seven rooms and added the Turquoise Café, where the floor is inlayed with the blue gemstones. He also commissioned Zuni artist Tony Edaakie to paint a series of murals depicting the Shalako (a series of dances and ceremonies the Zuni people conduct at winter solstice).

During its heyday, the De Anza Motor Lodge was listed in the *Negro Motorist Green Book*, a guidebook for African American road trippers published from 1936 to 1966.

The return of the De Anza Motor Lodge's sign along Route 66 signaled the renaissance of this historic motor lodge. Photo by Ashley M. Biggers.

DE ANZA MOTOR LODGE

What: Tony Edaakie murals
Where: 4301 Central Ave. NE
Cost: None
Pro Tip: Visitors may visit the murals only on guided tours. For more information, visit thedeanza.com or rt66deanza.org.

The lodge fell into disrepair after Wallace's death in 1993. The City of Albuquerque purchased the property a decade later and secured its spot on the National Register of Historic Places in 2004. However, the building sat derelict for thirteen more years before developers purchased it with the goal of rebuilding it into a Route 66 icon.

Jim Trump, president of Strategic Asset Management and construction manager, is overseeing the mixed-use redevelopment. He says preserving the murals was key. The developers went to great lengths to install proper ventilation, lighting, and fire suppression to protect the panels. They are working with members of the Zuni Pueblo to guide the public to see Edaakie's work. Meanwhile, there's a more visible way to appreciate this family of artists: Developers commissioned Edaakie's grandson, Keith, to paint a Rainbow Man mural on the exterior of one of the buildings.

MIDAS'S TOWER

Why was a city skyscraper gilded?

A glittering tower lights up the city skyline east of downtown. Now defunct architectural firm Flatow, Moore, Bryan, and Fairburn designed the First National Bank Building East. Standing seventeen stories tall, it was the tallest building in New Mexico when it was completed in 1963.

During construction, it was an eye-catching sight along Route 66. According to the *Albuquerque Tribune*, the "City Traffic Department had complained that motorists slowing to count the floors of the now-completed seventeen-story building were snarling traffic." The contractor solved the mystery by painting numeral signs on each floor to mark their progress while the building was under construction.

The building's twenty thousand square feet of gold ceramic tile also demanded attention. To keep the building cool, the architects clad the building with one-inch square gold tiles alternating with white concrete planes and gray heat-reducing glazing. The gold tiles catch the New Mexico sunlight, enhancing the city's post-World War II urban identity as part of the Sunbelt.

FIRST NATIONAL BANK BUILDING EAST

What: Golden building

Where: 5301 Central Ave. NE

Cost: None

Pro Tip: Harvey Hoshour, a notable Albuquerque modernist architect, designed a neighboring drive-up bank building. For more on Hoshour's influence, see page 6.

First National Bank Building East is covered in twenty thousand square feet of gold ceramic tile. Photo by Ashley M. Biggers.

The building was imagined as the cornerstone of a five-and-a-half block commercial campus; however, that development never materialized. The campus was a matched set with a concurrently built project in downtown Phoenix. Albuquerque's twin tower has since been remodeled and no longer bears any resemblance to the one in the Duke City.

The bank occupied offices in the building until the Great Recession of 2008. Today the New Mexico Department of Motor Vehicles and other state offices occupy the tower.

Although offices occupied most of the First National Bank Building East, the top two floors were devoted to the Albuquerque City Club.

FOUR-WAY STOP

Why does Route 66 intersect itself in Albuquerque?

Route 66, a.k.a. the Mother Road, is one of the country's most iconic highways. Beginning in 1926, it cut a 2,448-mile path across the country from Chicago, Illinois, to Santa Monica, California—but not always on the most direct path.

Route 66 grew out of the National Old Trails movement, which linked the east and west coasts via the routes Western pioneers traveled. When the federal government signed Route 66 in the 1920s, it picked up portions of the historic Santa Fe Trail. Early Route 66 drivers got their kicks along the Santa Fe Loop, which traveled from Santa Rosa to Albuquerque via Romeroville, Bernal, Pecos, Santa Fe, Santo Domingo, Algodones, and Bernalillo. Essentially, it took the long way around the Sandia Mountains' formidable peaks. It arrived in Albuquerque's downtown along Fourth Street.

After re-alignment in 1937, Route 66 followed the Santa Fe Cut Off, which shortened travelers' paths by taking them through Moriarty and Tijeras Canyon, then along Central Avenue. At the intersection of Fourth Street and Central Avenue, Route 66 meets itself at ninety degrees—the only place in the United States where it does so.

Albuquerque has the longest urban stretch of Route 66 in the country.

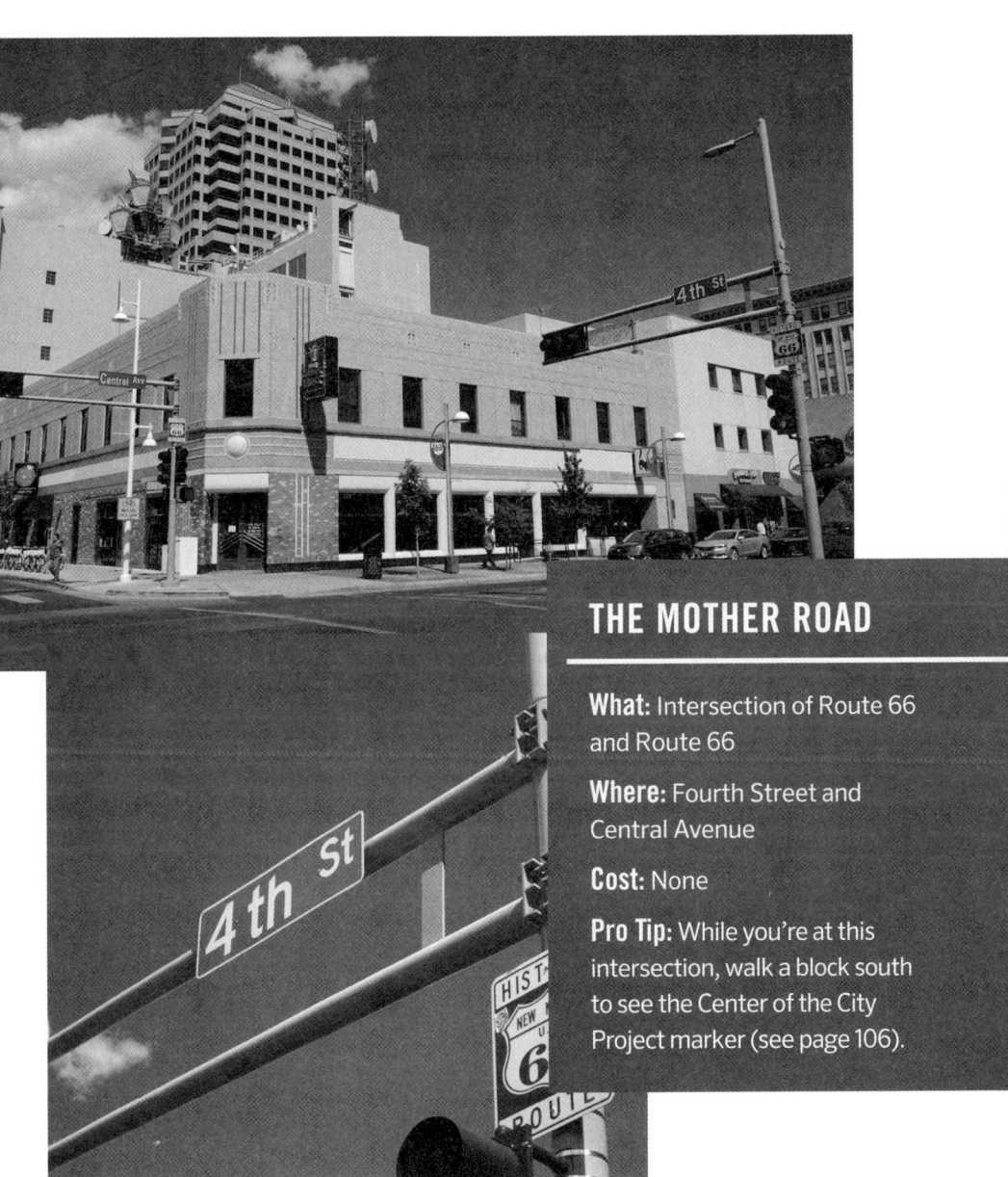

THE MOTHER ROAD

What: Intersection of Route 66 and Route 66

Where: Fourth Street and Central Avenue

Cost: None

Pro Tip: While you're at this intersection, walk a block south to see the Center of the City Project marker (see page 106).

Route 66 intersects itself at a ninety-degree angle at the corner of Central Avenue and Fourth Street in downtown Albuquerque. Photos by Nick Cessac.

GIDDY UP

Why was there an amusement park dedicated to Red Ryder in Albuquerque?

Red Ryder, a cowboy who battled bad guys with his young Native American sidekick Little Beaver, found fame as a character in a syndicated comic strip. The character went on to starring roles in comic books, a radio series, a TV series—and an Albuquerque amusement park.

Fred Harman, *Red Ryder's* artist, moved to Albuquerque from his native Pagosa Springs, Colorado, to be closer to a major airport to ship out the syndicated comic strips, which ran in seven hundred newspapers across the country from 1938 to 1965. It was one of the most popular cartoons in syndication history. Red Ryder has stayed in the cultural zeitgeist in the film *A Christmas Story*, in which the main character covets a Red Ryder BB gun.

Capitalizing on Route 66's growing motorist traffic, Harman dreamed up a roadside attraction devoted to his famous cowboy and trusty sidekick. Harman purchased land in Tijeras Canyon, near Route 66, for the attraction. In the planning phase, he called the amusement park First American Indian Land (with the rather unfortunate acronym FAIL), but he settled on Little Beaver Town.

Little Beaver Town opened to the public July 15, 1961. Amusement park guests would have seen a Western town, complete with the Red Bull Saloon, and an Indian village. There were five mock shootouts a day starring Dave Saunders, who brought Red Ryder to life, and Troy Vicenti (Jicarilla Apache), who played Little Beaver.

Little remains of what was once Little Beaver Town, an amusement park dedicated to the character Red Ryder. Photo by Ashley M. Biggers.

LITTLE BEAVER TOWN

What: Former *Red Ryder* amusement park

Where: East of the American Society of Radiological Technologists building (15000 Central Ave. SE). When driving east, look for a small parking pull-out and a gate on the right (south) side of the road. An Albuquerque Open Space sign marks the location.

Cost: None

Pro Tip: *Red Ryder* expert Roland Penttila, of the Albuquerque Historical Society, has guided tours of the Little Beaver Town site through the Albuquerque Open Space Division summer series. Check the schedule for offerings at cabq.gov/parksandrecreation/open-space.

The amusement park was short lived. By the end of the summer season in 1963, the park was a ghost town. Harman stopped drawing shortly thereafter and returned to Colorado. Today the site, which is part of Albuquerque Open Space, has a few hints of what was once there—a concrete slab where the Native American dances took place and ruins of the stucco buildings that once made up the Western town.

In 1962, Cliff Hammond operated Cliff's Amusement Park out of Little Beaver Town before that amusement park landed in its long-time location on San Mateo Boulevard.

AT&SF 2926 (page 170)

Photo by Ashley M. Biggers

CLYDE TINGLEY CHAIR (page 76)

Photo by Nick Cessac

THE RANGE CAFÉ (page 70)

Photo by Ashley M. Biggers

LUMBERJACK STATUE (page 110)

Photo by Nick Cessac

ARTISTIC FOSSILS (page 40)

Photo by Ashley M. Biggers

MAGGIE'S DINER (page 136)

Photo by Ashley M. Biggers

Photo courtesy of AMAFCA

TUMBLEWEED SNOWMAN (page 46)

PAINTED LADY BED & BREW (page 2)

Photo courtesy of Painted Lady Bed and Brew

Photo by Ashley M. Biggers

ORIGAMI IN THE GARDEN (page 152)

Photo by Ashley M. Biggers

ALBUQUERQUE ROLLER DERBY (page 134)

OCCIDENTAL LIFE BUILDING (page 174)

Photo by Nick Cessac

FRACTAL FOUNDATION'S BALLOON *INFINITUDE* (page 164)

Photo courtesy of Fractal Foundation

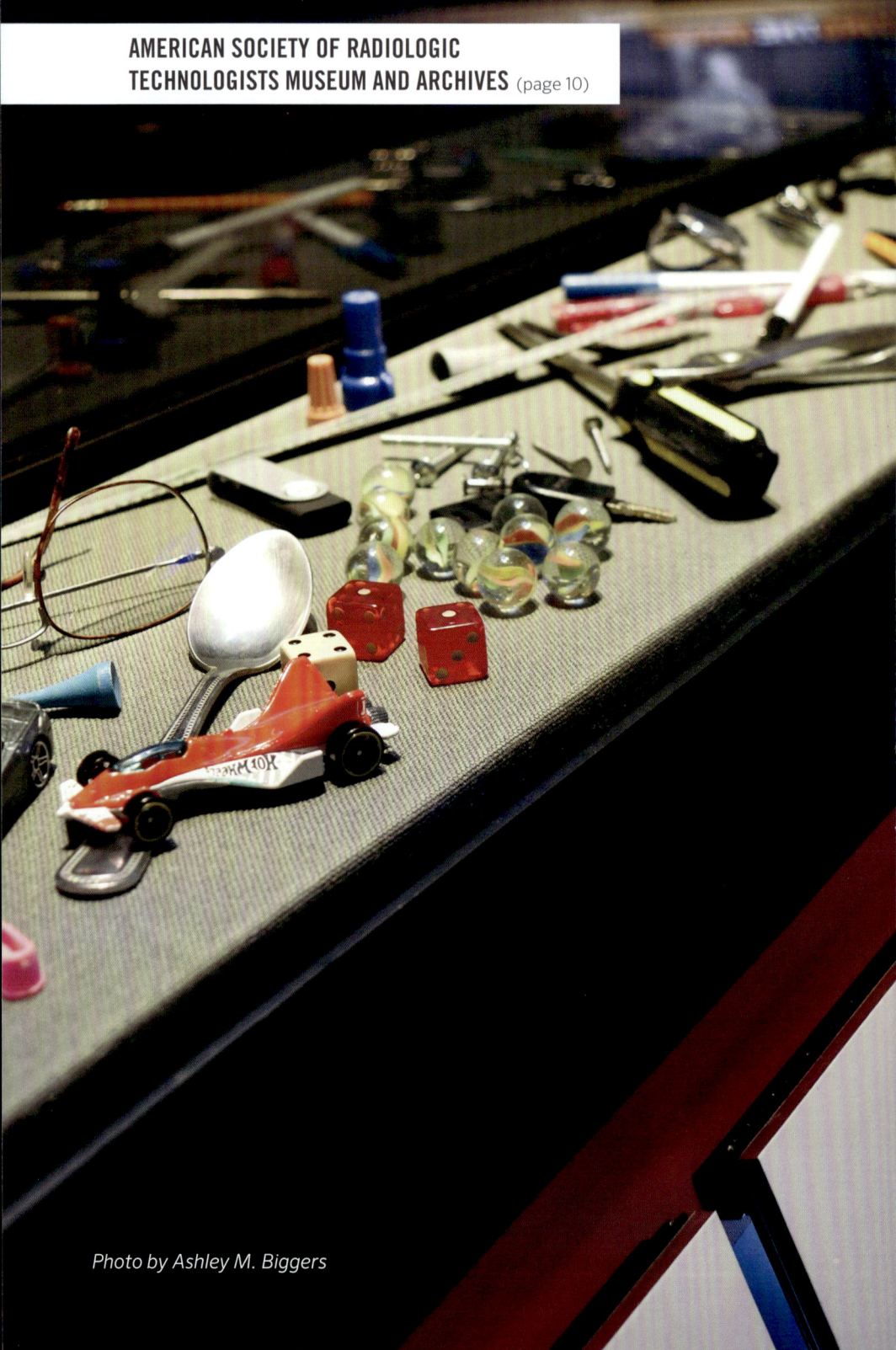

AMERICAN SOCIETY OF RADIOLOGIC TECHNOLOGISTS MUSEUM AND ARCHIVES (page 10)

Photo by Ashley M. Biggers

EYE OF THE SANDIAS (page 144)

Photo by Ashley M. Biggers

TINKERTOWN MUSEUM (page 158)

Photo by Ashley M. Biggers

SANTO NIÑO MISSION CHURCH (page 186)

Photo by Ashley M. Biggers

FIT FOR A PRINCESS

Why is Albuquerque home to storybook ranch homes?

When most people imagine Albuquerque, they immediately picture adobe (or adobe-style stucco) homes, but the Duke City has ridden several architectural style waves. In the 1950s, builder Dale Bellamah brought the storybook ranch style to a Northeast Heights neighborhood.

The son of a Lebanese immigrant, Abdul Hamid "Dale" Bellamah (1914–1972) helped build the American Dream for families searching for the picture-perfect post-World War II life with a house, yard, and car. He was determined to provide homes for the everyman at an affordable price. He mass-produced homes with small variations in finishes to achieve the dream.

The development's 1,600 homes capture a Disney-esque fantasy. They're painted in yellow, pink, and blue. Their roofs have exaggerated pitches and positions, including a butterfly roof where the roofline dips in the middle and rises to points on each side like a pair of wings. Many include cedar-shake shingles on the facades or are finished with scalloped barge boards reminiscent of a gingerbread house.

Princess Jeanne Park embodied 1950s suburban life so well that the Smithsonian's National Museum of American History featured it in a 1994 exhibit titled *Science in American Life*.

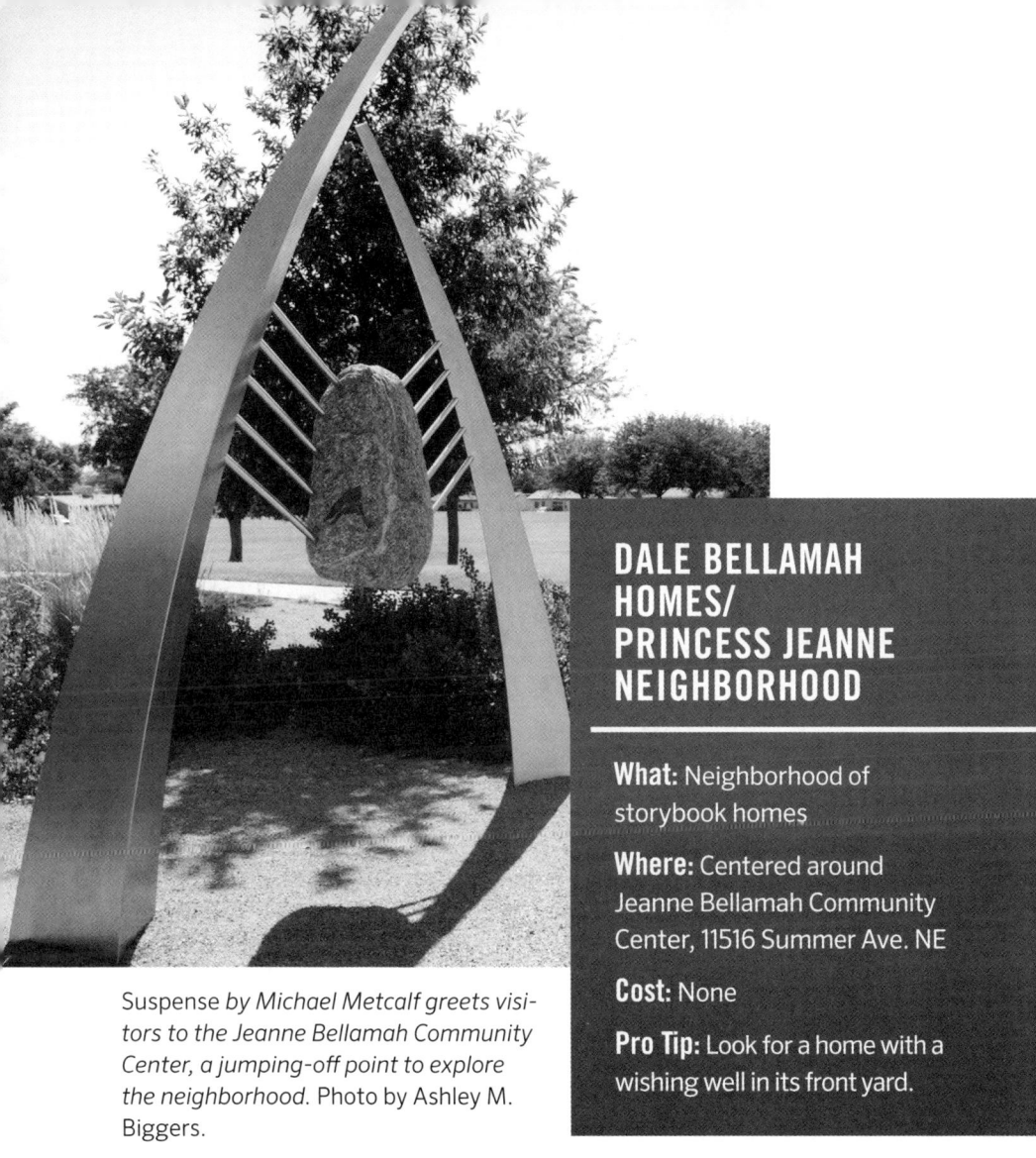

Suspense *by Michael Metcalf greets visitors to the Jeanne Bellamah Community Center, a jumping-off point to explore the neighborhood.* Photo by Ashley M. Biggers.

DALE BELLAMAH HOMES/ PRINCESS JEANNE NEIGHBORHOOD

What: Neighborhood of storybook homes

Where: Centered around Jeanne Bellamah Community Center, 11516 Summer Ave. NE

Cost: None

Pro Tip: Look for a home with a wishing well in its front yard.

Bellamah imagined the homes as "wife-planned" houses and named the development after his wife, Jeanne. Advertisements promised the houses would free wives from the "drudgery of household chores" with modern appliances, such as washing machines, refrigerators, and in-sink garbage disposals. Of course, these interior details aren't visible via a driving tour through the neighborhood, but many of the exterior details are.

MILE MARKERS

Where was the center of the city?

Two manhole-like medallions mark the locations of Albuquerque's geographic center in 1912 and 2012.

The public art project was a team effort. Then-*Albuquerque Journal* reporter Leslie Linthicum first wondered about the location of the center of New Mexico in 2008. Cliff Wilkie, City of Albuquerque geodetic surveyor, picked up the baton and located the center of Albuquerque shortly thereafter. They marked the location with black duct tape, but they felt there should be something more permanent in place.

City of Albuquerque Public Art stepped in. Sherri Brueggemann, manager of the Albuquerque Public Art Urban Enhancement division, suggested the markers be a pair: one marking the location of the city center in 2012 and one for a century earlier, when New Mexico became a state.

Yamilette Duarte created the artistic markers. Because they look much like manhole covers, they're easy to walk over and never notice. Yet the designs are intricate. The 2012 marker is the relief of the 1912 version; what's recessed in the 1912 marker is raised in the other. Duarte used repeating letter A's to suggest the name

---

The Center of the City Project emblems are made of cast iron from recycled City of Albuquerque manhole covers.

This marker is set at the location of Albuquerque's city center in 1912. Photo by Nick Cessac.

CENTER OF THE CITY PROJECT

What: Centennial markers

Where: 123 Fourth St. SW (in front of Amy Biehl Charter High School) and 301 McKnight Ave. NW (at Coronado Park)

Cost: None

Pro Tip: Visit the marker at Coronado Park during the day.

Albuquerque and to mark the cardinal directions. The outer circle has degree tick marks, just like a compass.

The site of the 1912 marker splits the distance between Old Town, where Albuquerque was founded in 1706, and New Town, where the railroad helped establish a new town site in 1891. It's also near the intersection of Fourth and Central avenues (to read more on this intersection, see page 82). The second marker isn't far afield, despite the city's rapid growth to the north. It sits at Coronado Park, 1.8 miles north of its sister.

WHERE'S ALDO?

Where did a grandfather of conservation live?

Author, ecologist, and conservationist Aldo Leopold is primarily associated with Wisconsin, where he was a professor. However, he spent several formative years in Albuquerque, living in a quaint home on Fourteenth Street.

Leopold first arrived in Albuquerque in 1909 for a position with the U.S. Forest Service Office. Assignments took him to Arizona and northern New Mexico, but he returned to the Duke City in 1914 to settle down with his wife, Estella. The homes in what is now recognized as the Aldo Leopold Neighborhood Historic District on the National Register of Historic Places were completed by 1920. In this home and during frequent trips to the river, Leopold formulated his early thoughts about land stewardship.

In 1917, Leopold took leave from the forestry service to work for the Albuquerque Chamber of Commerce. In that role, he proposed a riverside park along the Rio Grande that would protect rather than drain the wetlands. He saw preserving the forests as vital to both wildlife and people. He advocated for giving Albuquerque residents

---

After visiting Leopold's home, head to the Aldo Leopold Trail through the fifty-three-acre forest dedicated to the *Sand County Almanac* author. The forest extends from the Rio Grande Nature Center to the southeast side of the Montaño Bridge.

The grandfather of conservation, Aldo Leopold, lived in this home within walking distance of the Rio Grande Bosque as he solidified his ideas for a riverside park. Photo by Ashley M. Biggers.

a bit of fresh air and water within walking distance of their homes—the forest certainly is within walking distance of his. Although he moved to Wisconsin in 1924, the sentiment for preserving land along the river didn't leave with him. It took a while to germinate, but the Rio Grande Valley State Park was established in 1983, cementing the land ethic Leopold had planted.

ALDO LEOPOLD'S HOME

What: The conservationist's former house

Where: 135 Fourteenth St. SW

Cost: None

Pro Tip: This is a private home; conduct yourself accordingly.

TIMBER!

Why is there a giant lumberjack statue–at a Vietnamese restaurant?

When May Café owner Liem Nguyen repaired the fiberglass lumberjack that towers over his restaurant in Albuquerque's International District, he made headlines. The lumberjack's arms had blown off in a 2013 windstorm, and the giant had stood armless and ax-less for six years before he was restored to his former glory.

But why was he there in the first place? The lumberjack is a holdover from Shofner Lumber Co., which used to operate at that location. Anecdotally, the first lumberjack was installed in 1960 when Muffler Men (large molded fiberglass sculptures used to catch passersby's attention) were in vogue. The initial sculpture was replaced in 1974. The second lumberjack didn't start out that way. The sculpture was originally a chef, which lumber store owner Frank Shofner modified with clay and coated with fiberglass to look like a lumberjack.

Over the decades the lumberjack has become a neighborhood landmark. The Nguyen family wanted to preserve it—even if the lumberjack had nothing to do with

---

MAY CAFÉ LUMBERJACK

What: Giant lumberjack statue

Where: 111 Louisiana Blvd. SE

Cost: None to visit, meals vary

Pro Tip: Into lumberjack statues? There's also one at K&S Service Center (337 Eubank Blvd. NE). Abe Kreider Sr. commissioned the twenty-five-foot-tall lumberjack in 1971. It's carved out of a single tree trunk.

A towering lumberjack has presided over this location since 1960. It was originally a lumber store; today it's a Vietnamese restaurant. Photo by Nick Cessac.

Vietnamese cuisine. Repairing it involved using a hydraulic crane to reach the twenty-seven-foot sculpture on its twenty-foot platform. Restorers used steel reinforcements to repair his arms and ax, and they also gave him a fresh coat of paint.

> Cuban locals have nicknamed the lumberjack "Fidel."

A NEW TWIST

How did an inn get a monumental nautilus as an addition?

Don't call it a nautilus. At least not if you're talking to architect Bart Prince, who designed the curving form above the entry to what is now Casas de Suenos bed and breakfast. Prince, who is based in Albuquerque, is known for architecture inspired by organic forms. His creations have a knack for earning nicknames. His home and studio in Nob Hill, for example, is known locally as the "Spaceship House." The form at Casas de Suenos had a similar fate. The local landmark and photo op spot earned the moniker "The Nautilus." However, "I was *not* building a nautilus nor was I thinking of anything like that," Prince writes.

He designed the space in 1977 as a studio for Robert Hanna, an attorney who owned the property at the time. Prince was tasked with planning a sculptural addition to the existing faux-adobe building that could serve as Hanna's home studio. The shape resulted from the interior function. Hanna wanted a large office where he could work, as well as a space to set up his hobby photography studio. Hanna also commissioned a mural from California

---

Casas de Suenos has an artistic past: New Mexican painter and photographer Joseph Roy (J. R.) Willis (1876–1960) built the compound in 1938. It later became La Miradora house and apartments and was recognized as an artists' colony.

Bart Prince's design for a home studio at what is now Casas de Suenos has earned the nickname "The Nautilus." Photo by Ashley M. Biggers.

CASAS DE SUENOS

What: Monumental nautilus

Where: 310 Rio Grande Blvd. SW

Cost: None to spot it outside; stay from $199

Pro Tip: If you're staying at the bed and breakfast, ask to see the paintings by the home's original owner, J. R. Willis.

artist Greg Brown for the office's interior. Prince envisioned the space so the mural could flow continuously from the lower area, housing the photography studio, to the upper workspace. He wanted it to be visible while Hanna worked. The exterior curved structure, which does bear a striking resemblance to a nautilus shell, was finished in ceramic tile.

CREATIVE SPACES

How can you sleep inside a mural room?

Many people experience art in galleries or museum exhibitions—and those locales rarely if ever host overnight stays. At Nativo Lodge, however, guests sleep inside rooms painted by contemporary Native American artists. The rooms are immersive artworks. The artists paint murals on every wall, including those in the bathroom.

    The project began in 2013 with a set of four rooms. Heidi Brandow (Native Hawaiian/Diné), Nanibah Chacon (Diné), Rhett Lynch (Diné), and Ehren Kee Natay (Diné/Kewa Pueblo) painted the first set. The project has since expanded to forty-seven guest rooms.

    Each mural reflects the artist's particular inspirations. Many of the murals explore Native American cultures, spirituality, traditions, and heroes. For example, Lynch depicts a string of prayer pouches in the room Hózhó, while artist Cloudface (Diné) explores seasonal cycles through the symbol of the hummingbird in Arrival/Departure. In If You Believe, Michael Toya (Jemez Pueblo) intertwines traditional Puebloan designs with pop-culture influences in the form of *Star Wars* Stormtrooper masks. Depending on the room, the ambiance may be bold, alluring, or meditative, but it is always striking.

Nativo Lodge periodically hosts open houses so locals can tour the artist mural rooms.

The artist mural room Arrival/Departure, by Cloudface, captures the symbolic significance of hummingbirds in Diné culture. Photo courtesy Heritage Hotels and Resorts.

At Nativo Lodge, guests can sleep in artist mural rooms such as #1NDN by Ishkoten Dougi. Photo courtesy Heritage Hotels and Resorts.

NATIVO LODGE

What: Artist mural rooms

Where: 6000 Pan American Fwy. NE

Cost: From $96

Pro Tip: Nativo Lodge is popular during October's Albuquerque International Balloon Fiesta. If you're planning to stay during this time, book at least six months in advance.

ARTISTIC INTENT

Why did a sculpture earn headlines?

Luis Jimenez (1940-2006) found fame creating towering fiberglass sculptures depicting working-class people on both sides of the Mexican border. One of his most noteworthy works, the *Southwest Pieta*, was intended for installation at Old Town's Tiguex Park. However, neighborhood residents protested its placement because they believed the sculpture depicted an assault, and it was relocated to Martineztown. In spite of the controversy, President Clinton named the sculpture a national treasure in 1999.

Jimenez was born in El Paso, Texas, and grew up working in his father's commercial sign shop. He studied with muralist Francisco Zúñiga in Mexico City before finding success on his own in New York. In the 1970s, Jimenez returned to the Southwest, where he created monumental works for public squares and museums. In a tragic turn, one of these sculptures killed Jimenez when it fell on the artist while he was working in his studio in Arroyo Hondo, New Mexico.

Jimenez built the *Southwest Pieta* under the umbrella of the City of Albuquerque Public Art. According to the plaque describing the sculpture, it depicts the Aztec legend

---

SOUTHWEST PIETA

What: Sculpture by Luis Jimenez

Where: Southeast corner of Edith Boulevard and Roma Avenue at Martineztown Park

Cost: None

Pro Tip: While you're visiting the *Southwest Pieta*, see the Acequia Madre (see page 190).

According to sculptor Luis Jimenez, the Southwest Pieta *represents a warrior cradling a fallen maiden. In the Mexican folk tale that inspired the sculpture, the strength of their love transformed their souls into the form of volcanoes.* Photo by Ashley M. Biggers.

of Popocatepetl, a warrior, and Iztaccihuatl. The sculpture shows the moment in the legend when Ixtacihuatl dies. Overcome with grief, the warrior cradles the dead woman. It echoes Michelangelo's famous Renaissance sculpture, known simply as the *Pieta*, that depicts Mary cradling the body of Jesus after the crucifixion.

Jimenez also created the dancing figures of *Fiesta Jarabe* outside Popejoy Hall at the University of New Mexico.

A SIDE OF HOPE

How can a cup of coffee help people transition out of homelessness?

From the outside, Hope Café looks like any other museum café. Behind the scenes, there's much more than lunch prep taking place. Here, ordering a cup of coffee can help a person experiencing homelessness get a job and transition to a better situation.

Founded as an arm of HopeWorks, the Hope Café trains people who are experiencing homelessness (or near-homelessness) in the restaurant industry. The six-month training program teaches basic restaurant skills, from running the cash register to making espresso drinks to cooking and serving customers. It's considered an internship, and employees are paid and collect tips on a daily basis. At the end of their café training, the interns also receive resume writing and job search assistance. By graduation, applicants are prepared for entry-level positions within the restaurant and retail industries, says café manager Julie Yung. Throughout the program, the interns also work with other departments within HopeWorks, such as housing and therapy, to ensure they receive the support to be self-sufficient.

Founded in 1985, HopeWorks is the state's largest nonprofit organization working to end homelessness among individuals and families.

The Hope Café trains people who are experiencing homelessness or near homelessness in the restaurant industry. Photo by Ashley M. Biggers.

HOPE CAFÉ

What: Café that gives a leg up

Where: New Mexico Museum of Natural History & Science, 1801 Mountain Rd. NW

Cost: Varies

Pro Tip: If you encounter a long wait, grab a cookie or muffin to take away.

HopeWorks opened its first café, called the Coffee Shop, in 2011 at a different location. Hope Café moved into the New Mexico Museum of Natural History & Science in 2017. The partnership enabled HopeWorks to expand its program, going from three to ten to twelve interns at a time, and the museum gained a café operator. The café is also a social enterprise; revenues funnel back into HopeWorks programs.

GO WITH THE FLOW

Where can you see a volcano "explode"?

The volcanoes that frame Albuquerque's west side are known as the Three Sisters, but there's a fourth "volcano" on the horizon. The Albuquerque Metropolitan Arroyo Flood Control Authority (AMAFCA) built this volcano as part of a water diversion improvement project in 2017. Although it may fall short of full-on art, it is more exciting than the gray concrete channels that dominate the city's flood control efforts. Because the neighborhood is already home to extinct volcanoes, the board thought a volcanic cone would be fitting.

When the Duke City receives rain, water floods down the volcano's sides. It flows through channels lined with black and orange rock to make the water look like lava. Lights, which were installed in 2018, add to the illusion. If ever the volcano reaches full water flow, it will shoot water six feet in the air in a true explosion.

These LED lights' colors shift seasonally. On a normal day, the lights slowly change colors. At Christmas, they glow red and green. On the Fourth of July, they shine red, white, and blue. And on St. Patrick's Day, they illuminate with a lucky green.

The volcano serves a practical purpose: It oxygenates the water to make a healthier environment for fish—including the endangered silvery minnow—when the water flows into the Rio Grande.

When it rains, the AMAFCA volcano's overflow looks like lava; orange LED lights add to the effect. Photo courtesy of AMAFCA.

AMAFCA VOLCANO

What: Albuquerque's version of the Empire State Building

Where: The volcano is visible from the westbound I-40 off ramp at Ninety-Eighth Street.

Cost: None

Pro Tip: Head here when it rains to see the volcano working.

ART HUB

How can you connect with "low" culture?

Bianca Encinias may oversee El Chante: Casa de Cultura, but she'll be the first one to tell you it's a community effort. In 2010, she opened the doors to this gallery, library, and community workshop space. Art exhibits feature works from emerging artists with punk, ska, and New Mexico cultural styles. Two free libraries, Librotraficante Library, an intergenerational collection, and Le Plebe Children's Library, lend books in English and Spanish. And in the small downstairs shop, local artists sell oversized Zia earrings, rockabilly-style aprons with images of the Virgin of Guadalupe, and screen-printed jackets with dancing calavera (representations of human skulls associated with the Day of the Dead).

El Chante also hosts "low" culture events, including an annual low-rider gathering where the modified cars dip low for neighborhood cruises. Manuel Gonzalez, Albuquerque's poet laureate from 2016 to 2018, also teaches "low-writing" workshops twice a month. The performance poet represented Albuquerque four times as a member of the ABQ Slam Team at the National Poetry Slam. Everyone is

---

EL CHANTE: CASA DE CULTURA

What: Cultural center

Where: 804 Park Ave. SW

Cost: Varies

Pro Tip: If you want to listen instead of write, check El Chante's schedule of events. It also hosts poetry slams.

Former poet laureate Miguel Gonzalez teaches "low-writing" workshops at El Chante: Casa de Cultura. Photo by Nick Cessac.

welcome at the workshops on self-expression—even those who have never written poetry before. Workshops may focus on writing about emotions, such as anger, or may explore the poetry of place.

Alan Milne (a.k.a. A. A. Milne), writer of *Winnie-the-Pooh*, previously owned the home now housing El Chante: Casa de Cultura. Writing is in this building's roots.

NO BIG GULPS HERE

How did a gas station become a diner?

At Kellys Brew Pub, you can chow down on green chile cheeseburgers and craft beers next to a Texaco gas pump. It's a throwback to the building's roots as the Jones Motor Company.

Architect Tom Danahy designed the building for the Jones Motor Company, which had a gas station, car dealership, and repair shop, in 1939. The building enjoyed an enviable location at the intersection of Route 66 (Central Avenue) and Wellesley Drive, so motorists could drive up to gas pumps on two sides. With this in mind, it's no wonder owner Ralph Jones was a Route 66 booster. During the 1940s, he served as president of the Route 66 Association, president of Albuquerque's chamber of commerce, and chairman of the New Mexico State Highway Commission.

The building closed as a service station in 1957 and had stints as a Goodwill store and furniture mart. The owners of Kellys Brew Pub bought the building in 2000 and restored it. The eatery kept the building's signature Moderne-style façade, with a stepped tower and curved walls. They also preserved the building's garage doors and added gas pumps out front.

KELLYS BREW PUB

What: Eatery in a former gas station

Where: 3222 Central Ave. SE

Cost: Varies

Pro Tip: The Kellys patio is rollicking on summer Friday and Saturday nights.

Kellys Brew Pub preserved the Moderne-style façade from the original gas station and plays up its roots with vintage gas pumps on the patio. Photo by Nick Cessac.

The Standard Diner is also housed in a former gas station. It serves sophisticated comfort food in a 1938 Texaco station.

ALTERED STATES

Why does a local landmark have swastikas on it?

The KiMo Theatre is renowned for its Pueblo Deco architectural style. This style combines hints of Art Deco, the prevailing design when the 1927 picture palace was built, and Pueblo influences. These Pueblo influences account for what might strike some as an unusual detail: swastika symbols.

The KiMo's founder, Italian immigrant and businessman Oreste Bachechi, founded his business empire with a liquor establishment in a tent by the railroad tracks before venturing into the entertainment business. As his fortunes grew, he and his wife, Maria, envisioned a theater of their own. They hired Carl Boller, of Los Angeles-based architecture firm Boller Brothers, to design and build the KiMo. The final design included New Mexican influences, such as plaster ceiling beams mimicking grand vigas (ceiling beams), vents disguised as weavings, and thirty-five buffalo skulls with glowing red eyes. (No one's sure how Boller arrived at this particularly fearsome-looking detail, says KiMo manager Larry Parker.)

Boller also incorporated colorful Native American symbols, including swastikas. In 1927, before Nazi Germany co-opted and transformed the symbol, it was an ancient

---

Boller traveled through New Mexico's pueblos for months to research the KiMo Theatre's design.

The KiMo Theatre, an Albuquerque entertainment and architectural landmark, incorporates Native American symbols. Photo by Ashley M. Biggers.

KIMO THEATRE

What: Pueblo Deco landmark with Native American symbols

Where: 423 Central Ave. NW

Cost: Varies

Pro Tip: KiMo Theatre staff offer free guided tours twice a week. Check kimotickets.com for times and dates.

representation of life, the changing of the seasons, and prosperity. Many Southwestern tribes hold the symbol sacred, though different tribes assign slightly different meanings. The Hopi see it as a symbol of wandering tribes, while the Diné consider it a whirling log (*tsil no'oli*). It was with these positive meanings in mind that Boller inscribed the symbol on what is now a prominent city landmark.

A 1963 fire destroyed much of the original stage. It was painstakingly restored, including all the original symbols, during the landmark's restoration.

YOU'RE GOING TO NEED MORE CLAMPS FOR THAT

How did a twelve-story wood and glue structure help win the Cold War?

Dr. Carl E. Baum oversaw the construction of the ATLAS-I (short for Air Force Weapons Lab Transmission-Line Aircraft Simulator) between 1972 and 1980 at Kirtland Air Force Base. Nicknamed the Trestle after the railroad bridges that inspired its design, the ATLAS-I helped Baum and his team test how aircraft would react to the electromagnetic pulses released by nuclear detonation.

The Trestle is a thousand feet long and stretches six hundred feet (twelve stories) above the desert. The $60 million structure was built using very little metal. It's made of pine and fir logs, as well as glue and fiberglass bolts. All the materials are invisible to electromagnetic pulses.

From 1980 to 1990, Baum and his team towed military aircraft, such as bombers, onto the wooden deck and bombarded them with EMPs similar to those made by an exploding nuclear bomb. The top-secret experiments measured the pulses' effects on the aircraft's electronics. Of course, they didn't use actual nuclear blasts. They

---

The Trestle is regarded as one of the world's largest wooden structures.

The ATLAS-I (a.k.a. the Trestle) sits on Kirtland Air Force Base. You can't get a look up close, but you can spot it in the distance from the Sandia Mountains foothills (in the left of this image). Photo by Ashley M. Biggers.

charged the deck with Marx capacitors with 0.2 terawatts of electricity.

The Trestle was retired in 1991 when safer and less expensive computer models could do similar work. The Trestle has sat abandoned since.

ATLAS-I

What: Cold War wooden structure

Where: The ATLAS-I is located on Kirtland Air Force Base. Visiting it up close is impossible; see the Pro Tip below.

Cost: None

Pro Tip: The ATLAS-I is visible from the Sandia Mountains foothills, including the trail to the Eye of the Sandias (see page 144).

TO THE WALL

Why does Albuquerque have a piece of the Indianapolis Motor Speedway?

Drivers along Montaño Boulevard can easily spot a section of concrete wall and caging from the Indianapolis Motor Speedway. The wall is straight out of the Unser family's racing history. In 1989, Al Unser Jr. was speeding his way to his first Indianapolis 500 win. He was battling Emerson Fittipaldi for the lead when the drivers' wheels touched. Unser spun out and hit the wall—this wall. As Fittipaldi cruised past under caution, Unser climbed out of the wreckage and gave a "thumbs up" sign. That wasn't Unser's year, but he would go on to win that famed race two times. He was also inducted into the Indianapolis Motor Speedway Hall of Fame in 2007. And Al Unser Jr. is just one member of the Unser racing family; together they share nine Indy 500 wins. So when the Brickyard swapped out its wall for one that better protected spectators, it offered this historical section to the family for its Albuquerque museum.

The Unsers arrived in Albuquerque in 1936. Al Unser Sr.'s father, Jerry, and his uncles had begun their driving careers competing in the Pikes Peak International Hill Climb. However, when Jerry couldn't find work during the Great Depression, the family headed south to the Duke City. Jerry found work in an auto garage. He opened his own mechanic shop in 1940, which cemented Albuquerque as the family's hometown.

This section of wall outside the Unser Racing Museum came directly from the Indianapolis Motor Speedway. Photo by Ashley M. Biggers.

The Unser Racing Museum chronicles the family's early racing days and career milestones. The memorabilia include a replica of the (borrowed) car Al Sr. drove to his fourth and last Indy 500 win in 1987. Other items include numerous original race cars and pace cars from Indy 500 wins, and the family's uniforms.

UNSER RACING MUSEUM

What: Racing memorabilia

Where: 1776 Montaño Rd. NW, Los Ranchos de Albuquerque

Cost: $10 for adults

Pro Tip: Don't miss the museum's second building. It has even more cars, including antique and classic cars from Al Sr.'s personal collection.

The museum also exhibits two-of-a-kind "Goodstone" team shirts that Al Sr. and his wife, Wanda, made when their sons drove for the Goodyear and Firestone teams and they wanted to support both.

WRITTEN IN STONE

Why does a boulder bear a mysterious inscription?

In the 1920s, a rock in the Los Lunas area, south of Albuquerque, began earning international acclaim for its enigmatic origins. The rock, often called the Mystery Stone or the Decalogue Stone, is inscribed with a CliffsNotes version of the Ten Commandments in a language that was initially thought to be either a form of Paleo-Hebrew or Cypriot Greek. In either case, that would have implied these groups had been wandering New Mexico's high deserts in ancient times.

Trust land archaeologist David Eck has the real story. In the 1920s, a ranch hand discovered the inscribed stone and took acclaimed archaeologist Dr. Frank Hibben there to see it. Hibben wrote a news article about the find, though he fell short of proclaiming it real. The rock achieved near instant cult status as people made pilgrimages to the stone and posited theories about its source, which even included ancient aliens etching the text.

According to Eck, the stone's likely origin is far more pedestrian. While the inscription does indeed relate the Ten Commandments, it isn't rendered accurately, which led Rabbinic scholars investigating the stone to pronounce it a hoax. In fact, it is a copy of a text widely available in libraries during the 1920s. Eck wonders if students from

---

> Eck says he believes Dr. Hibben appreciated a good joke and likely found the "mystery" surrounding the stone amusing.

The Mystery Stone has inspired several tales suggesting it has ancient origins, but the modern-day editing marks you'll find on its surface suggest a more recent creation. Photo courtesy of New Mexico State Land Office.

> ### THE MYSTERY STONE
>
> **What:** Stone with enigmatic origins
>
> **Where:** The Mystery Stone is located on New Mexico State Land. Visiting the site requires getting a recreational access permit. Directions to the site are issued with the permit.
>
> **Cost:** $35 for permit
>
> **Pro Tip:** There is legitimate prehistory on the way to and around the stone. Walk softly.

the University of New Mexico etched the passage as a joke. "Clearly they were not paying attention because they missed the second statement," he says. "They went back and stuck it in between their otherwise evenly spaced statements, even using a modern editor's caret mark to insert the missing line." Vandals later damaged the first line of the inscription, bludgeoning out the phrase's mention of a deity (though they missed a subsequent mention of the deity later in the inscription).

Why has the mystery continued? Eck offers one answer: "People want to believe. What they want to believe is anyone's guess. As soon as they believe, they stop thinking."

SKATING ALONG

Where can you see roller derby?

At the whistle, they're off—slowly. Teams of roller skaters, their arms linked in Red Rover–fashion, glide around a track. The jammer, with her star-emblazoned helmet cover, begins maneuvering to get around the blockers. It looks like a rugby scrum, but on roller skates. Suddenly the jammer breaks free. In a sudden flurry, she sails around the track, trying to lap the opposing team. It's just another night of roller derby in Duke City.

There are more than a thousand amateur roller derby leagues worldwide, and Albuquerque is home to two of them: Duke City Roller Derby, an all-women's league, and Albuquerque Roller Derby, which has co-ed teams. The latter was founded in 2015 and has aspirations of creating a team sanctioned by the Women's Flat Track Derby Association, the international governing body of this full-contact sport for women. Albuquerque Roller Derby's team, the Unicorns, competes against teams in Texas, Colorado, and Arizona in four to five home bouts during its April to November season.

The sport had a short-lived Hollywood turn in the roller derby flick *Whip It* (2009) starring Ellen Page, and in some ways the movie rings true in real life. The

---

Roller derby skaters go by nicknames. The Unicorns roster has included Ivy Nightmare, Jurney, and Metal Mayden.

The jammer breaks through the blockers at an Albuquerque Roller Derby bout, one of four to five home bouts held each year. Photo by Ashley M. Biggers.

Albuquerque Unicorns are a team of tough people who take the competition seriously. However, their bouts have a playful, family-friendly atmosphere—as their faces painted with rainbows and glitter attest. "In roller derby, there are all shapes and sizes. All skill levels," says Unicorns team member Katie Jurney. "We have bankers, X-ray techs, and authors. I launch rockets for a living. It's a very inclusive community."

ALBUQUERQUE ROLLER DERBY

What: Off-the-beaten-path sport

Where: Bouts are usually held at the Manuel Lujan Jr. Exhibit Complex at Expo New Mexico, 300 San Pedro Dr. NE.

Cost: $10

Pro Tip: The Unicorns also have a youth team, the Narwhals, for seven- to seventeen-year-olds.

MOVIE MEMORIES

How did a former movie set become a t-shirt shop?

Family flick *Wild Hogs* (2007) filmed many of its scenes in the Albuquerque area. The Country Club neighborhood doubled as Ohio, where the film's protagonists lived. In the story, the four middle-aged friends (played by Tim Allen, John Travolta, Martin Lawrence, and William H. Macy) hit the road on motorcycles headed for California. They run afoul of the motorcycle gang Del Fuegos in a small town in New Mexico. The town of Madrid, in the East Mountains, was the backdrop for these scenes. Many of the filming locations are real. Maggie's Diner, a central location in the film, however, was built exclusively as a film set.

The production leased land from Hugh and Honoree Hacket, owners of the Great Madrid Gift Emporium, who happened to have a bit of spare acreage in the otherwise wall-to-wall town. Santa Fe County code required that the set be built as though it were a real building—no false walls or unsupported structures here.

After filming wrapped in 2006, the Hackets set about turning the set into a working building. Because of town water and parking covenants, they weren't able to turn Maggie's into a real diner. The Hackets settled on a

---

MAGGIE'S DINER

What: Souvenir shop on a movie set

Where: 2867 N.M. 14, Madrid

Cost: Varies

Pro Tip: While you're at Maggie's, stop by the Great Madrid Gift Emporium next door for turquoise jewelry.

Maggie's Diner was built as a movie set for Wild Hogs. *It's become a pilgrimage site for motorcycle riders.* Photos by Ashley M. Biggers.

souvenir post, which opened in 2008. The shop has become a pilgrimage site for motorcyclists, who grab their selfies outside before heading inside to shop for *Wild Hogs* t-shirts and Harley-Davidson head scarves.

Maggie's Diner is a must-see for motorcycle tour groups traveling across the country on Route 66. In the height of the summer, several hundred riders a day might stop at the shop.

A SUBURB OF ONE'S OWN

Where is Albuquerque's first African American neighborhood?

Today, an easy-to-miss, dilapidated sign marks the location of the East End Addition. It's the home of Albuquerque's first African American suburb.

Henry Outley founded the neighborhood. He homesteaded a 160-acre ranch near what is now the intersection of Wyoming and Lomas boulevards. Outley was an airport janitor and owned a boarding house on Stover. In 1924, the entrepreneur partnered with Dr. James Lewis (the second African American doctor in the Duke City) to open the Booker T. Washington Sanatorium on Arno Street. Outley was entrepreneurial in other ways, too. He and the Fraternal Aid Society, an association of black businessmen of which Lewis was also a member, wanted to make suburban life a reality for people of all races.

In 1938, Outley platted 144 acres of his homestead into a subdivision that would have included seven blocks' worth of homes, plus a large green space called Outley Park. However, because of redline laws that prevented homes from being sold to Asian or African American people, he wasn't able to move forward with the development. He

Many of the homes have been torn down; the neighborhood is pushing for historic preservation to protect the rest.

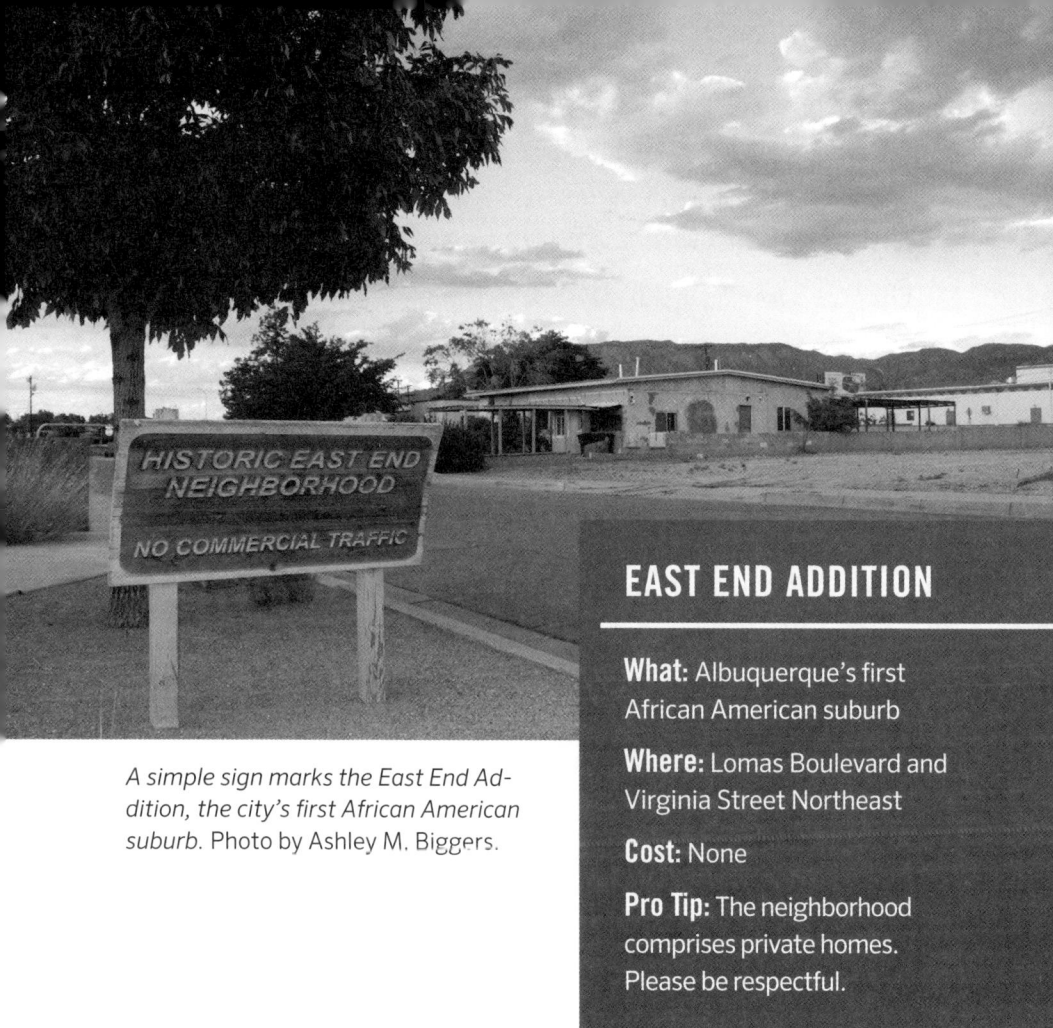

A simple sign marks the East End Addition, the city's first African American suburb. Photo by Ashley M. Biggers.

EAST END ADDITION

What: Albuquerque's first African American suburb

Where: Lomas Boulevard and Virginia Street Northeast

Cost: None

Pro Tip: The neighborhood comprises private homes. Please be respectful.

instead deeded the East End Addition to his daughter, Virginia Outley Ballou.

She had her own business—a barbecue restaurant that is said to have catered in the households of Ben Abruzzo and William Lovelace—but took up her father's mantle when she saw African American servicemen being denied use of their G.I. Bill loans on homeownership after World War II. Working with J. S. Jones, an African American architect and builder from Phoenix, she built between sixteen and thirty-one homes between 1950 and the 1980s. (Accounts differ on the number of homes built.) Some early residents, including ninety-seven-year-old Oscar Jones, still call the neighborhood home.

COMING HOME

Where did Jim Morrison live as a child?

Jim Morrison (1943–1971), a.k.a. the Lizard King and Mr. Mojo Risin, was the lead singer for the Doors. His poetic lyrics and distinctive voice in songs such as "Light My Fire" and "Break on Through (to the Other Side)" captivated fans and made him an iconic front man. His dramatic death, at age twenty-seven, cemented his mystique. The rock legend lived in Albuquerque during his formative years.

His father, George Morrison, served in the U.S. Navy and at the Naval Special Weapons Facility at Kirtland Air Force Base from 1955 to 1957. (Young Jim Morrison wrote that he wanted to kill his father in the hit "The End.") Jim Morrison lived in Albuquerque from ages twelve to fourteen and attended Monroe and Wilson middle schools.

During that time, Morrison allegedly saw an incident that influenced his songs and poetry. As described in his biography *No One Here Gets Out Alive*, Morrison witnessed a car accident in the desert involving a Native American family in which some members were injured and others killed. The Morrisons later moved to Alexandria, Virginia.

Morrison fans are pushing to preserve his childhood home as a historic site.

This ranch-style house once housed rebellious rocker Jim Morrison. Photo by Nick Cessac.

JIM MORRISON'S HOME

What: The Doors' front man's former home

Where: 8912 Candelaria Rd. NE

Cost: None

Pro Tip: This is a private home. Please be respectful.

Thelma Lue, who owns the Morrisons' home in the Northeast Heights, wonders whether Jim ever left. She's heard organ music coming from his former bedroom. She says she doesn't mind fans stopping by.

CHEERS TO PROHIBITION

Where can you get a drink at a former bootlegger's bar?

Before opening Silva's Saloon in Bernalillo, Felix Silva Sr. was a bootlegger. He hid his still in the middle of an apple orchard and the liquor bottles beneath his car floorboards as he ran moonshine all the way to Oklahoma. He went (mostly) legit in 1933 when he opened Silva's Saloon along the original stretch of Route 66.

Even after opening the bar, Felix Sr. didn't entirely give up his bootlegging ways. Felix Silva Jr. says his father sold on Sundays and to Native Americans even though laws then prohibited doing so. Felix Silva Sr.'s original fruit press, which he used to juice apples for brandy, and his copper still from the 1920s sit in a corner of the bar.

Over the decades, the saloon has become a time capsule. Magazine articles, photos, cowboy hats, and signed dollar bills litter the walls and bar shelves. The collage tells the story of the bar's history and its patrons' lives. The patrons have left permanent marks here, too: Felix Jr. points out blood on the ceiling from 1949, when Felix Sr. used a pipe to keep a bar patron in line. The bar

---

Felix Sr. passed away in the bar in 1995—and his spirit may have stuck around. Felix Jr. feels that his dad plays tricks on him.

Silva's Saloon was founded by Felix Silva Sr., a former bootlegger. If he's working, Felix Silva Jr. will tell you all about his father when you stop in for a drink. Photo by Ashley M. Biggers.

SILVA'S SALOON

What: Bar founded by a bootlegger

Where: 955 S. Camino Del Pueblo, Bernalillo

Cost: Varies

Pro Tip: Ask Felix about the phone booth he keeps in operation because it was used in a real-life spy drama in the 1990s.

shelves have become vaults, too. A row of seventy-year-old bottles of whiskey runs along a top shelf. They're sealed with wax and opened only for special occasions.

A SIGHT TO BEHOLD

How can you visit an enigmatic painted symbol in the mountains?

The Eye of the Sandias is well known among those who frequent Sandia Mountains trails; however, it's virtually unknown to those who don't venture there often. The Eye of the Sandias is a mural of an eye on a boulder high in the foothills.

An unknown artist painted the quirky, three-foot-by-three-foot landmark sometime in the 1960s. Persons unknown have touched up the symbol over the years. The stylized Eye looks a bit like the Egyptian Eye of Horus, which symbolizes protection, power, and good health. A Zia, the symbol of New Mexico, sits in the pupil's center. The Eye has tears dripping from the corner. Urban legend suggests the Eye represents the mountain's sadness at the city's encroachment. It may also be meant as a symbol of protest against development.

Reaching the Eye requires a 3.8-mile round-trip hike. The hike gains around 1,200 feet in elevation over the 1.9-mile trail, which is rated moderate to difficult depending on the source. The final climb to the Eye is quite steep. This vantage overlooks Tijeras Canyon to the south and the entirety of Albuquerque to the west.

Unknown artists also painted a large pair of turquoise feet on boulders near the Eye.

The Eye of the Sandias is a New Mexico version of the Eye of Horus; it has a Zia symbol painted in the pupil. Photo by Ashley M. Biggers.

EYE OF THE SANDIAS

What: Mysterious painted eye

Where: Hike departs from a parking lot at the eastern terminus of Copper Avenue. Precise trail directions are available online and in area hiking guides.

Cost: None

Pro Tip: This is an exposed trail. Pack plenty of water and be prepared for a climb.

GONE BUT NOT FORGOTTEN

What famous figures are buried in a historic cemetery?

Fairview Memorial Park is a microcosm of Albuquerque and New Mexico history. The historic cemetery, now tucked between the University of New Mexico and the Albuquerque International Sunport, was once a sandy hill on the city's outskirts where the bereaved laid their family and friends to rest—though unofficially. The first recorded burial at what would become Fairview Memorial Park was Mary Josephine Perea, an infant who died on February 27, 1881. The family's monolithic headstone also memorializes the death of her brother, Mosheim, in 1889.

The historical section of the cemetery, which includes nearly twelve thousand burials, sits at the north side of the park. The three sections include a Victorian area with burials from 1881 to 1908 (around which time the cemetery became official). The Congregation Albert Cemetery began in 1902, and a more modern section developed by the Strong family, long-time park caretakers, started in the 1930s.

Several notable Albuquerqueans are buried here, including Edmund G. Ross (1826–1907), who served as New Mexico's territorial governor from 1885 to 1889.

There are more than four dozen cemeteries in Bernalillo County.

Fairview Memorial Park is the final resting place of some of the city's most prominent former residents. Photo by Ashley M. Biggers.

FAIRVIEW MEMORIAL PARK

What: Historic cemetery
Where: 700 Yale Blvd. SE
Cost: None
Pro Tip: Visit the cemetery during the day.

As a Kansas senator, in 1868 he cast the deciding vote that kept President Andrew Johnson in office when Johnson was impeached for high crimes and misdemeanors.

Other notable headstones include those of U.S. representatives Ruth Hanna McCormick Simms and Albert G. Simms. The widow and widower met when serving in Congress for Illinois and New Mexico, respectively. After they married, McCormick Simms relocated to New Mexico, where she and her husband established their ranch and dairy at Los Poblanos (see page 182), among other endeavors. McCormick Simms's son, John "Johnny" Medill McCormick, is also interred at the park. McCormick's story gripped the nation in 1938 when the heir to the *Chicago Tribune* went missing for eight days. The twenty-one-year-old and a friend had gone hiking. When they failed to return, McCormick Simms organized a search party to scour the Sandia Mountains. The bodies of both men were found near an area known as the Shield. They'd apparently been struck by lightning. McCormick Simms had the boulder where they found her son's crumpled body moved to the cemetery to lie in front of his gravestone.

PARQ IT

How did a former railroad and psychiatric hospital become a hotel?

The Atchison, Topeka & Santa Fe Railway Hospital opened in 1926 to much fanfare. It was designed to treat the railway employees who had been flooding into the Duke City. In the 1940s, the hospital changed its name to the AT & SF Hospital. In the 1980s, it lost its railroad connections altogether when a group of psychiatrists purchased it to run an inpatient facility and dubbed it Memorial Hospital. By the 1990s, the hospital was falling into disrepair, but it didn't officially close until 2007.

The building got a second life when it was reborn in 2010 as Hotel Parq Central. The hotel kept the Italianate-style architecture but otherwise bears little resemblance to its former self. Today it's a sophisticated, modern boutique inn.

Ghost hunters thrill at the thought of the countless people who must have passed away there during the building's hospital days. Anecdotally, the children and teens who were patients of Memorial Hospital noticed paranormal activity. They reported their bedsheets being pulled off during the night, being covered in scratches, and hearing voices.

A few tongue-in-cheek references hint at the hotel's past, such as a coffee table that uses a hospital gurney as the base.

Though it's been renovated, Hotel Parq Central kept the railroad hospital's original Italianate-style façade. Photos by Nick Cessac.

HOTEL PARQ CENTRAL

What: Former railroad and psychiatric hospital

Where: 806 Central Ave. SE

Cost: Stay from $140

Pro Tip: Grab a drink at the rooftop Apothecary Lounge.

STUFFED

What restaurant serves a seven-pound burrito?

Grandma's K&I Diner serves the Travis on a Silver Platter, which weighs in at an astonishing seven pounds. The behemoth burrito takes three flour tortillas to wrap around the pinto bean and ground beef filling. It's smothered in red and green chile sauce, topped with cheese, tomatoes, and lettuce, and then—as though that wasn't sufficiently filling—piled high with fresh, hand-cut French fries. Diners can take on the Travis on a Silver Platter challenge and get the twenty-four dollar burrito for free if they eat it in under an hour. When the Travel Channel show *Man v. Food* featured the Travis on a Silver Platter in 2001, then-host Adam Richman called the challenge an "indomitable feat of manhood." However, it should be pointed out that a woman is among the handful of diners who have conquered the monstrous burrito.

Irene Warner opened Grandma's K&I Diner in 1960. She named the restaurant after herself and her daughter, Kay Hess. She owned and operated the eatery until her death in 1999, when her daughter took it over. When Kay passed away in 2018, the restaurant changed hands again. The

---

> When the Travis on a Silver Platter was featured on the Travel Channel's *Man v. Food* in 2011, the host recruited three men named Travis to take on the challenge. None conquered it.

Grandma's K&I Diner is home to the legendary Travis on a Silver Platter. Photo by Ashley M. Biggers.

GRANDMA'S K&I DINER

What: Home of the seven-pound burrito

Where: 2500 Broadway Blvd. SE

Cost: $24, free if you eat it in an hour

Pro Tip: Can't manage a Travis on a Silver Platter? Opt for a quarter-Travis. It's the most popular version.

mystical tale of the sumo-wrestler-sized burrito has been lost over the years. Local folklore has two versions. In the first, a family friend named Travis stopped by the restaurant starving. The cooks were busy with customers, so Irene told him to go in the kitchen and make himself something. His creation became known as the Travis. In another version, a mysterious visitor, perhaps a truck driver, stopped in and asked for a burrito with everything but the kitchen sink. The cooks delivered just what he asked for. Regardless of how it began, the Travis is worthy of the legend.

CRANING TO SEE

Why is there monumental origami in the East Mountains?

Along N.M. 14 on the Sandia Mountains' eastern façade, metal points jut from the piñon-studded landscape. The sculptures capture the delicate folds of origami cranes, horses, and butterflies in steel, bronze, and aluminum. Artists Jennifer and Kevin Box created the exhibition, called *Origami in the Garden*. The show has both monumental and fundamental sizes. Since 2015, it has traveled the country to Ohio, Illinois, Minnesota, and Florida, to name a few. But each summer it lands in the Boxes' five-acre front yard in Los Cerrillos. Gentle nature trails wind through the high desert, leading to a dozen or so pieces from the show.

Originally a paper artist and graphic designer, Kevin Box took a trip to Greece, where sculpture captured his artistic attention. He changed gears but never lost his fascination with paper. The lost-wax casting process, which enables his designs to begin as paper but become cast metal, unified his vision. After a New Mexico trip packed with serendipity, the Oklahoma artist found both a new home and a creative and life partner in his now-wife, Jennifer.

ORIGAMI IN THE GARDEN

What: Monumental sculptures in the high desert

Where: 3453 N.M. 14, Los Cerrillos

Cost: None

Pro Tip: Tours are offered weekly on Fridays when the garden is open.

Crane Unfolding *by Kevin Box introduces visitors to* Origami in the Garden, *a show of metal sculptures mounted in the East Mountains each summer.* Photo by Ashley M. Biggers.

    The Boxes collaborate with origami artists such as Michael G. LaFosse, a master of the intricate art of paper folding, to render works such as *Emerging Peace*, which depicts the transformation from a caterpillar to a butterfly. The Boxes co-created *Master Peace*, a tower of five hundred cranes. Completing the Japanese tradition of folding a thousand cranes, the Boxes made another five hundred crane sculptures that are now winging their way around the world to private and public collectors.

Origami in the Garden is on view from Memorial Day through the Albuquerque International Balloon Fiesta in October.

BURGERS AND THRIFT STORE FINDS

Where can you peruse antiques while you eat?

The Grill restaurant could be a set for *Antiques Roadshow*. Saws, license plates, photos of military service members (including owner Phil Chavez), and an emblem from an REO Speed Wagon truck are just a few examples of items strewn across the walls. "I just love antiques and old things," Chavez says. "This place is like a Cracker Barrel and a Fuddruckers combined."

Chavez was serving in the Navy when he first started learning the restaurant business in 1988. While visiting his uncle in Santa Rosa, California, he fell in love with the restaurant Jalisco Mexican Food. He worked for free to learn everything he could. Once out of the Navy, Chavez returned to his hometown of Gallup, New Mexico, where he opened his own Mexican restaurant. Over the years, he set aside the hours of prep required in a from-scratch Mexican eatery for easier-to-prepare fare: burgers. He opened his first burger joint in one end of his father's former auto garage in Gallup and decorated it with antiques pilfered from the barn at his family's ranch. The Grandpa's Grill chain came to Albuquerque about a decade ago. It's been at its current location, where it goes by

---

The Grill prepares burgers on a mesquite-wood-fired grill.

The collection of vintage pieces and antiques on the walls of the Grill includes everything from old license plates to Western bridles. Photo by Ashley M. Biggers.

simply the Grill, for the past three years.

Some of the wall antiques are from Chavez's family. Others are items he's picked up at garage and estate sales, or at thrift stores. Recently, customers have started bringing him items to help decorate. In 2019, one brought him an entire firefighter's uniform. The walls have sections devoted to automotive items; firefighters and law enforcement; military service members; Western items; and sports, music, and movie memorabilia. Chavez's favorite item is a Marine officer's sword from the 1940s. You can spot it while you're chowing down on your burger.

THE GRILL

What: Restaurant with memorabilia

Where: 3300 San Mateo Blvd. NE #B2

Cost: Varies

Pro Tip: Head to the build-your-own-burger bar for all the fixings.

GOING GREEN

Why does Albuquerque have a hidden park?

To locals, McDuffie Park is known as Hidden Park. The three-acre green space certainly earns its moniker. It's sandwiched between houses in Nob Hill, with many houses' backyards backing up to the park. Short alleys lined with concrete-block walls lead to the grassy expanse. It's possible to drive right by and miss the passageways into the park. The park itself is a relatively typical one, with elms, cottonwoods, and oaks shading the lawn below. However, it has gained a following thanks to its oasis-like atmosphere.

The City of Albuquerque Parks and Recreation Department isn't sure how McDuffie Park landed in obscurity. Nob Hill subdivisions were built between the 1920s and 1950s. It's possible the developer felt obligated to include this space—even if sandwiching it in. Since the department was founded in 1954, an ordinance has required that all new developments include park space.

The practice of shoehorning green spaces is typical in Nob Hill, which is dotted with small green spaces tucked among homes and triangle "parks" at intersections. These commons are usually less than an acre in size, some as small as a third of an acre. They include Hermosa Green Park (826 Parkland SE) and Beyer Park (801 Grandview

---

Albuquerque has the most parkland per capita in the United States.

The secluded entrances to McDuffie Park earned it the nickname "Hidden Park." Finding the lush green space is well worth the effort. Photo by Ashley M. Biggers.

MCDUFFIE PARK

What: Hidden park

Where: 3708 Mackland Ave. NE

Cost: None

Pro Tip: Check out the Little Free Library station at the north end of McDuffie Park.

SE) near Carlisle Place; Monroe Green Park along Pampas Drive; Vail Park (4607 Eastern SE); Ross Park (4809 Crest SE); and Eunice Kalloch Park (1201 Quincy SE).

GLASS HOUSE

Why is there a building made of fifty thousand glass bottles in the East Mountains?

It's rare to see the inner workings of an artist's mind. But that's exactly what it feels like to wander the carnival funhouse–inspired hallways and rooms of Tinkertown Museum. Folk artist Ross Ward grew up in the Midwest, where he was fascinated from an early age with those who carved figures in their spare time. He began carving his first miniature figures for what became his general store diorama in 1962. The self-taught artist spent more than thirty years as a painter with carnival shows before landing in New Mexico.

Inspired by Grandma Prisbrey's Bottle Village in California and Howard Finster's Paradise Garden in Georgia, he turned his two-room home into a twenty-two-room altar to folk art. The museum opened in 1983. He spent more than forty years collecting the fifty thousand glass bottles cemented into the property's walls, as well as the Old West paraphernalia and road-culture relics crammed into every corner of the maze-like structure. Visitors can have their futures predicted by a fortune-telling machine (just like in the film *Big*) and hear Otto,

---

The exhibits at Tinkertown Museum include everything from the shoes and pants of a former World's Tallest Man to a full-size sailboat docked in the woods.

Ross Ward spent decades carving the miniatures that make up the sixty-foot-long Western diorama. It is on display, along with many other creations, at Tinkertown Museum. Photo by Ashley M. Biggers.

the automatic one-man band, play. They can peer at tens of thousands of hand-carved figures, including an entire miniature Wild West town that stretches sixty feet long, and walk on license plates nailed to the floor.

Ward passed away in 2002. His wife, Carla, now oversees the museum.

TINKERTOWN MUSEUM

What: Folk artist's creations and collections

Where: 121 Sandia Crest Rd., Sandia Park

Cost: $4 for adults

Pro Tip: Tinkertown Museum is open late March through October. Check online for opening and closing dates. Bring quarters or get change at the admissions desk to operate the mechanical toys.

FORGOTTEN VILLAGE

Why is a kiva disappearing?

Tijeras Pueblo is often overlooked—even by pueblo completists. People flock to see dances at thriving pueblo communities and archaeological sites with standing evidence of dwellings. At Tijeras Pueblo, however, there's very little to see above ground.

The landscape obscures the two-hundred-room U-shaped village. Windswept mounds dotted with tufts of dried grama grass are the few hints at Ancestral Puebloan dwellings beneath the surface. People lived here from 1313 to 1425 AD; some speculate these families were part of the Four Corners migration that left sites such as Chaco Culture National Historical Park and Mesa Verde National Park empty.

Plastic stakes driven into the sand mark the shape of a large circular kiva, one of several found here, and serve as reminders of the excavation that took place from 1971 to 1976. The University of New Mexico Department of Anthropology excavated one-third of the pueblo, removing chipped-stone artifacts, pottery, animal and plant remains, and human skeletal remains. After they completed their

---

TIJERAS PUEBLO ARCHAEOLOGICAL SITE

What: Pueblo mounds

Where: 11776 NM-337, Tijeras

Cost: None

Pro Tip: The pueblo sits directly behind the Sandia Ranger Station. If time allows, stop by the on-site museum to learn more about the peoples who once dwelled here.

A circle of rocks and stakes in the ground mark where a large circular kiva once stood at Tijeras Pueblo Archaeological Site. Photo by Ashley M. Biggers.

work, they backfilled the site to protect it from erosion and looters.

The wind caused this pueblo's and its large kiva's disappearing act. Over the six hundred years since its occupation, sand has piled against walls and filled in floors, leaving only the occasional rocks to suggest something more underneath. At some point, the desert will reclaim those rocks too, leaving no visible trace of the village.

A third-of-a-mile nature trail winds among the pueblo mounds at Tijeras Pueblo Archaeological Site.

MOUNTAIN MEMORIAL

How can you hike to a plane crash site?

On February 19, 1955, TWA Flight 260 took off from the Albuquerque airport for a quick jump to Santa Fe. It never arrived. Seven minutes after take-off a warning bell sounded, indicating that terrain was close. The pilots saw the Sandia Mountains' sheer western face just beyond the plane's wing tip. Unable to turn in time, they collided with the granite face, killing all sixteen people aboard. After a contentious investigation into the cause, the Civil Aeronautics Board determined that faulty navigational instruments caused the crash.

The plane crashed in a remote area amid snowdrifts, so it took some time to locate the site. Rescuers braved freezing temperatures to reach the location. They quickly discovered it would be a recovery effort, not a rescue mission. They removed the bodies of those who perished but left much of the plane wreckage behind. Sections of a wing, tires, and the plane's engine are visible in the brush. Today from this location, hikers can hear the Sandia Peak Tramway soaring overhead.

Reaching the site requires a nearly eight-mile hike and around a 1,400-foot elevation gain. Before setting

---

Under certain conditions, usually in the winter when vegetation is sparse, the TWA 260 crash site is visible from the Sandia Peak Tramway.

The TWA 260 crash site is still littered with plane parts. Photo by Mike Coltrin.

A commemorative medallion was laid in the debris field to honor those who lost their lives in the crash. Photo by Mike Coltrin.

"TWA CANYON"

What: 1955 plane crash site

Where: Domingo Baca Trail. Turn-by-turn hiking directions are available online and in local hiking guides. (See bibliographical info.)

Cost: None, but parking fee may be required

Pro Tip: Please do not remove any items from the area. Treat this site with the respect due the people who lost their lives here.

out, make sure your fitness and preparedness match this hike's requirements. The trail begins in the Elena Gallegos Picnic Area and makes its way into the Sandia Mountain Wilderness along the Domingo Baca Trail.

MATH ALOFT

Why does Albuquerque have flying fractals?

Among the five hundred hot-air balloons floating in the Duke City's skies during the Albuquerque International Balloon Fiesta, two in particular catch visitors' eyes. *Infinitude* and *Fibonacci* have swirling fractal (never-ending patterns) designs. Both are the creations of the Albuquerque-based Fractal Foundation, which for almost two decades has brought attention to fractals and inspired interest in the intersections of science, math, and art.

Jonathan Wolfe, Fractal Foundation executive director and lead pilot of Duke City–based *Infinitude*, says, "Balloons are a powerful and inspiring symbol—of dreams, imagination, wonder, and magic. And the fractal-art balloons symbolize even more: they represent the infinite beauty of algebra, which creates the incredibly beautiful fractal patterns printed on the balloons."

Jared Tarbell, a visual artist who co-founded Etsy, and his wife, architect Laurie Tarbell, entirely funded *Infinitude*. They also donated a powerful computer necessary to calculate the complex imagery on this balloon's massive envelopes as well as others in the future.

> Fractals are everywhere in Albuquerque. With public fractal art, the First Friday Fractals and Fractals Rock! shows, and its fractal balloons, the Duke City claims the title as fractal capital of the world.

The Fractal Foundation's balloon Infinitude *teaches about the beauty of math wherever it flies.* Photo by Tania Goldfeder, courtesy of Fractal Foundation.

INFINITUDE AND FIBONACCI

What: Fractal hot-air balloons

Where: For flying times and locations, see fractalfoundation.org or follow the balloons on Instagram @FlyingFractals.

Cost: Varies

Pro Tip: You can spot fractal designs on the ground, too. Albuquerque Fractal Challenge winners' creations wrap buildings around the city. Locations include the New Mexico Museum of Natural History & Science, Harwood Art Center, and a parking structure at Third Street and Silver Avenue.

The Fractal Foundation inflates the balloons at public schools across Albuquerque to demonstrate how exciting and beautiful math can be. It also flies the balloons at Albuquerque International Balloon Fiesta each October. It plans to add more hot-air balloons to the fractal fleet.

TACO TUESDAYS, SOPAIPILLA SATURDAYS

What's a tacopilla?

For many New Mexicans, Grandma's cooking is the apex of cuisine. So Abuelita's New Mexican Kitchen sets high expectations with a name that, for many, recalls chile-laden dishes simmering on the stove and served around the family dining table. The restaurant's motto evokes these memories, too. It's a familiar *dicho* (saying): "Panza llena, corazón contento" or "full belly, happy heart."

The homey restaurant has earned praise thanks to a recipe passed down from Lucy Romero, the restaurant's founder. And, yes, she's really the abuela of Rubi Martinez, who owns the Albuquerque restaurant location.

Lucy's star recipe is the tacopilla, a portmanteau of "taco" and "sopaipilla" and a combination of these dishes. A plate-sized sopaipilla serves as the dish's foundation. It's folded over and filled to overflowing with refried beans, lettuce, tomatoes, guacamole, and sour cream, as well as a meat filling of choice, such as shredded beef, ground beef, or chicken. Because it's folded over, it does resemble a taco—though it's definitely the BFG of tacos.

> Abuelita's also prepares traditional New Mexican Lenten specialties, such as tortas de huevo and quelites.

The plate-sized tacopilla is a taco-sopaipilla hybrid. Photo by Ashley M. Biggers.

Although cooks make the recipe with sopaipilla (puffed fried bread) dough, there's some argument as to whether the behemoth is truly a sopaipilla. It's closer to a buñuelo, which is essentially a flat, Frisbee-sized sopaipilla that looks like Indian fry bread. Whatever it's called, it's delicious.

ABUELITA'S NEW MEXICAN KITCHEN

What: One-of-a-kind taco

Where: 6083 Isleta Blvd. SW

Cost: $10

Pro Tip: Abuelita's also has a Bernalillo location; it's under different ownership. It can be found at 621 South Camino Del Pueblo, Bernalillo.

SLITHERING SIGHTS

Why do enormous rattlesnakes slither?

Most people try to avoid rattlesnakes, particularly in Albuquerque where hikers encounter them on trails and residents often find them slinking through backyards. But drivers en route to the Isleta Amphitheater can't evade them. Along University Boulevard and leading to the Mesa del Sol entrance, a pair of monumental, two-hundred-foot-long rattlesnake sculptures dip in and out of the medians.

The City of Albuquerque hired landscape architecture firm Sites Southwest to create interest along these medians. The challenge? Sites Southwest didn't have access to any water in this neck of the desert. Senior landscape principal George Radnovich and his team decided on a sculpture and, more specifically, a rattlesnake, which is perfectly adapted to its desert environs.

Biologists quibble that the cobblestones covering the statues' bodies aren't the correct colors for true rattlesnakes. The stones do, however, mimic the snakes' mottled skin pattern. Their six-foot-tall heads have

---

RATTLESNAKE SCULPTURES

What: Gigantic rattlers

Where: Go east on Rio Bravo from I-25. Turn south on University Boulevard, toward Isleta Amphitheater. Follow it up the hill. If you park and walk to the sculptures, do so carefully.

Cost: None

Pro Tip: If you want to see real-life rattlesnakes, check out the American International Rattlesnake Museum in Old Town.

This rattlesnake is two hundred feet long, and its head is six feet tall. Good thing it's made of cobblestone. Photos by Nick Cessac.

become popular Instagram photo backdrops. Although urban legend has it that the snakes represent jilted lovers, Radnovich scoffs at the story.

Sites Southwest has also contributed to landscape design at Tiguex Park, Bachechi Open Space, and ABQ BioPark.

LOCO FOR LOCOMOTIVES

Where are volunteers restoring a railroad engine?

When railroad enthusiasts decided to rescue an engine and tender sitting derelict in Coronado Park, they thought they'd throw a fresh coat of paint on it and get it into working condition. Little did they know. In 2000, they purchased the car from the City of Albuquerque for a dollar. The restoration effort has taken two decades and cost $3.5 million. Volunteers have put in some two hundred thousand hours of work. And the locomotive isn't ready to run yet.

The AT&SF 2926 was placed into service on May 9, 1944. The engine and tender stretch 121 feet long, making it one of the largest locomotives in existence. The engine hasn't been in use since the 1950s, and it sat deserted in Coronado Park for decades. Many Albuquerqueans remember childhood days spent clambering up the locomotive's eight-inch-tall drive wheels and sitting in the conductor's chair.

The restoration effort began with laying track to move the locomotive from the park to the current worksite on Eighth Street. Now at a permanent worksite, the New Mexico Steam Locomotive & Railroad Historical Society,

---

The 510,150-pound AT&SF 2926 locomotive was built to barrel down tracks at ninety miles per hour.

The restoration of the AT&SF 2926 has been a DIY project of massive proportions. The volunteers have taught themselves to repair and even build parts for the 1944 steam engine. Photo by Ashley M. Biggers.

the organization behind the restoration, welcomes the public to observe. Knowledge of how to build and repair steam engines, such as the 2926, died with the railroad men who once worked on them. "None of the guys working had restored an engine before," says Mike Hartshorne, NMSL&RHS president. The NMSL&RHS has pieced together how to repair and rebuild the engine from old books, museums, and even mechanical drawings purchased on eBay. They can't exactly run to the local hardware store to find the parts they need, so they've had to build many of them at an on-site machine shop and foundry.

The volunteers aim to have the AT&SF 2926 working under its own power by the end of 2019. In the future, it will be used for the railroad equivalent of Sunday drives and excursions across the Southwest.

AT&SF 2926

What: Locomotive restoration

Where: 1833 Eighth St. NW

Cost: None, donations appreciated

Pro Tip: Visitors are welcome at the site Wednesdays and Saturdays, 9 a.m. to 2 p.m. Because work may stop in foul weather, call ahead to ensure the site is open: (505) 246-2926.

171

PUCK DROP

Where can you watch hockey from the ice?

Recreational skaters and amateur hockey players have been enjoying the Outpost Ice Arenas rinks since the 1980s. The company began with a single rink and added a second rink a dozen years ago. It connects these rinks with two curling tunnels, which create the CooLLoop. In 2019, it underwent a $2 million renovation to prepare for the arrival of the New Mexico Ice Wolves, a North American Hockey League team. And that unique CooLLoop enables it to sell on-ice game tickets. Spectators may watch games from the curling tunnels, which are on the same level as the rink where the game is played. Players thud into the board and skid to stops at eye level. It's a thrilling, one-of-a-kind spectating experience.

For a high-desert town, Albuquerque has a large hockey community built by transplants from out of state and even former European pro players who have retired in the Duke City. The city had been home to hockey teams previously, but it had been a decade since it hosted a professional or professional-track team. The NAHL New Mexico Ice Wolves play in a junior hockey league sanctioned by USA Hockey. Players may choose to play in the NAHL rather than playing in college as they attempt to be drafted into the professional leagues.

The CooLLoop creates a fifth-of-a-mile ice-skating track.

OUTPOST ICE ARENAS/NEW MEXICO ICE WOLVES

What: On-ice hockey viewing

Where: 9530 Tramway Blvd. NE

Cost: $10

Pro Tip: Arrive early to get your skates. The ticket includes a skate rental.

Thanks to curling tunnels connecting its rinks, the Outpost Ice Arenas offer on-ice tickets to New Mexico Ice Wolves games. Photo by Ashley M. Biggers.

DUKE CITY'S DOGE

Why does Albuquerque have a building that looks like the Doge's Palace?

Along with the KiMo Theatre, the Occidental Life Building is one of downtown's most unique architectural landmarks. If the Gothic Revival architecture reminds you of Italy more than Albuquerque, that's no mistake.

The building's original owner, A. B. McMillan, who founded the Occidental Life insurance company, admired the Palazzo Ducale, or the Doge's Palace, on a trip to Venice. He endeavored to create his own version stateside. He hired Henry C. Trost (1860–1933), of El Paso architecture firm Trost & Trost, to design the building. Trost is considered to have shaped Albuquerque's downtown skyline more than any other architect. Trost had a particular fondness for mimicking Italian buildings; however, in most cases style followed function. In this case, style led the design. The building's classic Gothic lancet arches, quatrefoil windows, and leafy ornamental motifs are lifted directly from the Doge's Palace. The striking white building is covered with glazed terra cotta tile.

Trost designed several other notable Albuquerque structures, including the First National Bank Building, the Sunshine Building, and the Rosenwald Building. The Occidental Life Building was one of the last buildings Trost designed.

The Doge's Palace inspired the Occidental Life Building's Venetian-Gothic design. Photo by Nick Cessac.

In April 1933, the building fell victim to arson and was gutted in the aftermath. Its original cornice was destroyed, but in 1934 architecture firm Brittelle & Ginner replaced the original with an ornamental frieze along the roofline that even more closely resembles the building's Venetian inspiration.

OCCIDENTAL LIFE BUILDING

What: Albuquerque's Doge's Palace

Where: 301 Gold Ave. SW

Cost: None

Pro Tip: While you're visiting, check out the site of the city's first balloon ascension (see page 30).

CULTURAL NEXUS

Where does a historic Elks Lodge have a new life as a barbecue joint?

In the 1950s, when some Albuquerque residents were enjoying social clubs across the city, African American residents had only one place to gather: the Navajo Elks Lodge. It was the only place they could socialize and party in the Jim Crow era. The Navajo Elks Lodge was a fixture in the South Broadway community for decades.

Johnny Goodwin joined the Elks in 1975. He DJed for the club's parties on Friday and Saturday nights for more than three decades. He describes the parties more as gatherings and family potlucks. They were open to anyone, Goodwin says, but for the African American community the space was unique.

In 2016, when aging members could no longer maintain the property, the lodge moved to another location. Ken Carson, a former banker who had left the corporate world to open Nexus Brewery, bought the building to ensure it remained accessible to the African American and South Broadway communities. Carson also grew up in the neighborhood. He employs several people

---

NEXUS BLUE SMOKEHOUSE

What: Barbecue in a historic building

Where: 1511 Broadway Blvd. SE

Cost: None

Pro Tip: Nexus has three locations across the city, including a brewery (4730 Pan American Fwy. NE) and taproom (2641 Coors Blvd. NW).

The Nexus Blue Smokehouse was once the Navajo Elks Lodge—one of the only places in the Duke City where African American residents could gather to dance. Photo by Ashley M. Biggers.

from the area, protecting the joint's neighborhood feel. Goodwin is one of the restaurant's most popular employees.

The menu includes favorites from Nexus's first location, including chicken and waffles, ribs, hot links, pulled pork, and smoked meats. Nine of the brewery's craft beers are on tap, as well as rotating seasonal offerings.

Nexus Blue Smokehouse serves New Mexican soul food. Don't miss the red-chile barbecue sauce.

A DIFFERENT KIND OF CLEANSE

Why does a shop have a "maggot pit"?

Michael O. Wieclaw is known for his irreverent, playful art. Under the umbrella of Metal The Brand, he designs New Mexico–themed t-shirts with Zia symbols made of burgers and fries, and pins shaped like tighty-whities proclaiming "Vivan los chones" ("Long live underwear"). His creations are local artists' market staples.

When he opened a brick-and-mortar store at El Vado Motel in 2018 called Metal The Shop, he saw the chance to fulfill a lifelong dream. "Ever since I was a little kid, I've always wanted to create a pit of decay," Wieclaw says.

That pit of decay is the art installation *Metal The Swamp*. A quasi-ball pit (like those at children's play places) is the centerpiece. This pit, however, is not filled with plastic balls. It overflows with custom-made molded plastic maggots. Wieclaw encourages visitors to "Come baptize yourself in decay in hopes the maggots will eat away [your] toxicity and infection." Sinking into the pit feels comforting in a way. The mass of maggots buoys you as though you're sitting in a custom-made chair,

---

Metal The Store is housed at El Vado Motel. The landmark 1937 hotel welcomed Route 66 travelers for decades. After renovation, it reopened in 2018 with a hotel, shops, and restaurants.

In the art installation Metal The Swamp, *visitors can sit in a pit with custom-made plastic maggots.* Photos by Nick Cessac.

letting you lean back to take in the fantastical, stuffed creatures in the pit with you and the vines overhead. These looping tendrils are branches of the Forgiving Tree; free stickers often dangle from the branches, ready for the taking.

METAL THE STORE

What: Home of the maggot pit

Where: 2500 Central Ave. SW, Suite AS4

Cost: None

Pro Tip: While you're at the store, take home a Duke City–themed t-shirt.

THAT'S A STRETCH

Where is New Mexico's longest bar?

At forty feet long, the Mine Shaft Tavern's lodge-pole pine bar is the longest stand-up bar in the state. Miners enjoyed bellying up to the bar after spending days hunched over in the coal mines surrounding what is now the town of Madrid.

Coal mining began in what was then known as Coal Gulch in 1835. At the time, it was a company town—in other words, the mining company owned everything, including the tavern, which opened in 1895. With that birthday, the tavern is in the running for the oldest in the state.

However, the original building burned down on Christmas Day in 1944. It was rebuilt and reopened in 1947. The interior remains much the same today—except for the dollar bills, which patrons have signed and plastered onto the walls over the years.

The mines closed in the 1950s, and the entire town went up for sale. It sat nearly empty for a couple of decades before artists and members of the counter-culture movement adopted it as their new hometown in the 1970s.

Madrid has been described as a former ghost town; the description may still fit in a different way. The Mine

---

The Mine Shaft Tavern was a filming location for the TV drama Longmire. *After filming the pilot here, the production built a set that replicated the historic bar.*

MINE SHAFT TAVERN

What: New Mexico's longest bar

Where: 2846 N.M. 14, Madrid

Cost: Varies

Pro Tip: Madrid is nationally known for its Christmas parade. If your plans allow, don't miss it.

The Mine Shaft Tavern is home to the longest stand-up bar in the state. Photo by Ashley M. Biggers.

The Mine Shaft Tavern has been serving drinks and good times since 1895. Photo by Ashley M. Biggers.

Shaft Tavern is said to be haunted. Patrons and servers have observed glasses falling from shelves and doors opening, and they've heard mysterious sounds.

The most frequently heard sound today, however, is the live music in the tavern and neighboring cantina. There customers can dine on the patio next to a non-working steam engine, which is part of the museum also on site.

CHISELING HISTORY

Where did Gustave Baumann carve wood beams and doors?

German artist Gustave Baumann (1881–1971) was a museum-collected printmaker and painter who led the American color woodcut revival movement. His works have been shown at the Metropolitan Museum of Art and the National Gallery of Art, and they are part of the New Mexico Museum of Art's permanent collection. (He lived in Santa Fe County for more than fifty years.) Most people are accustomed to seeing his woodcut prints, but his actual woodcuts are rarely seen. And rarer still are interior design pieces such as wood beams and doors, which he carved for Congressman Albert G. Simms and Ruth Hanna McCormick Simms.

The Simmses owned what is now Los Poblanos Historic Inn & Organic Farm. The property included an eight-hundred-acre ranch and a private residence that served as the headquarters for their cultural endeavors. In 1932, Ruth hired prominent Southwest architect John Gaw Meem to design La Quinta Cultural Center, a quasi-public structure. In turn, she and Gaw Meem commissioned WPA artists to detail the structure. Baumann carved

---

Los Poblanos's collections also include seven photographs by Laura Gilpin, one of the most important photographers of the American Southwest. The WPA photographer captured Los Poblanos's buildings and gardens.

Gustave Baumann is known for his woodcut prints; his large-scale wood carvings are lesser known. Photos by Ashley M. Biggers.

floral and Native American patterns in the massive pine doors of La Quinta's library and music room and the ceiling beams. He also carved a scene depicting San Ysidro, the patron saint of farming, over the mantel in the ballroom. Although the carvings are distant from his prints, they bear some of the geometries of his woodcuts. Los Poblanos is an uncommon opportunity to see his woodcarvings up close.

LOS POBLANOS HISTORIC INN & ORGANIC FARM

What: Gustave Baumann woodcarvings

Where: 4803 Rio Grande Blvd. NW, Los Ranchos De Albuquerque

Cost: Varies

Pro Tip: Join an art and architecture tour ($10) to get a behind-the-scenes look at the Baumann woodcarvings and more of Los Poblanos's treasures. For times and dates, see lospoblanos.com.

LUCY, WE'VE GOT A STAR

How did Vivian Vance start her career in Albuquerque?

In the 1955 *I Love Lucy* episode "Ethel's Home Town," the comic foursome of Ricky, Lucy, Ethel, and Fred take a Route 66 road trip to Ethel's fictitious hometown, Albuquerque. But this episode wasn't pure Hollywood fiction. Vivian Vance (1909–1979), who played Ethel Mertz on the hit TV show, started her career in the Duke City.

Vance was born in Oklahoma, but in 1929 her family moved to Albuquerque, where they hoped the dry air would help her mother's asthma. Vance's family ran the Vance Market downstairs in a 1910 redbrick building at Broadway Boulevard and Coal Avenue and lived upstairs. The building is now known as the Broadway Market Building.

Vance acted in her first show at the Albuquerque Little Theatre in 1930. Spotting her talent, the theater community raised money in 1932 to fund her way to New York City, where she could try to make it on Broadway. In the 1940s, Vance relocated to Los Angeles. She was performing at La Jolla Playhouse when Desi Arnaz spotted her talent and cast her as the frumpy sidekick to Lucille

---

THE BROADWAY MARKET BUILDING

What: Vivian Vance's childhood home

Where: Corner of Broadway Boulevard and Coal Avenue

Cost: None

Pro Tip: To see where Vance got her start acting, check out a performance at the Albuquerque Little Theatre.

Vivian Vance, who famously played Ethel Mertz in I Love Lucy, *lived above the Vance Market in what is now the Broadway Market Building.* Photo by Nick Cessac.

Ball's character in *I Love Lucy*. Even after becoming a star, Vance maintained her Duke City connections. She helped plan productions at the Albuquerque Little Theatre and donated money to build the theater's balcony.

Vance won an Emmy Award for best supporting actress in a television series in 1954; she was the first recipient of the award. Following her death in 1979, the family donated her Emmy to the Albuquerque Little Theatre.

GENERATIONS OF GENÍZARO

How can you visit a historic settlement of detribalized Native Americans?

New Mexico has an oft-cited tri-cultural heritage—Native American, Hispanic, and Anglo. History, and people, are rarely so easily categorized. In 2007, the New Mexico State Legislature passed a resolution recognizing the existence and importance of a little-known indigenous group: the genízaro. The designation was given to Spanish Colonial-era peoples and their descendants who are of Native American descent but adopt Hispanicized culture.

The first genízaro came from a variety of pueblos, the Diné, and the Comanche, to name a few. However, they lived among the Spanish as slaves (though the laws of the day required slaves to be freed at adulthood if they accepted Catholicism), servants, or day laborers. They adopted Spanish surnames from their masters and Christian names through baptism, spoke Spanish, and in some ways followed Spanish cultural practices.

In the mid-eighteenth century, the Spanish asked for genízaro volunteers to establish defense settlements around the Villa de Alburquerque. They aimed to protect

---

Genízaro also petitioned to establish settlements in the Albuquerque area as part of the Nuestra Señora de los Dolores de Belén and San Antonio de las Huertas land grants.

Descendants of the genízaro founders of Carnuel dance Los Matachines on San Miguel Feast Day. Photo by Ashley M. Biggers.

CARNUÉ

What: Genízaro community

Where: Santo Niño Mission/Holy Child Church, 7 Herrera Loop, Carnuel

Cost: None

Pro Tip: Community members dance Los Matachines near the Catholic feast day for San Miguel, on September 29. The dance is held at the mission church.

the villa against attacks from nomadic tribes such as the Diné, Ute, Comanche, Apache, and Kiowa. Genízaro families accepted because doing so presented the opportunity to become landowners and escape servitude. Families of these backgrounds established the community of San Miguel de Loredo de Carnué in Tijeras Canyon in 1763.

To travelers speeding at seventy-five miles per hour on I-40, Carnuel, as it's known today, is a blur of homes. However, the community has a rich history and cultural traditions passed down from its founders. The community recognizes its complex heritage with the dancing of Los Matachines, a ceremonial dance that tells the story of the intimate relationship between La Malinche, a Tlaxcala Indian maiden, and conquistador Hernán Cortés.

UNIVERSAL VIEWS

Where are the stars on view?

The Planetarium at the New Mexico Museum of Natural History & Science is on a well-trodden path. However, the University of New Mexico Campus Observatory, which is open to visitors for viewing sessions, is lesser known. Built in 1955, the observatory opened its doors to the public in 1963.

Undergraduate students open the dome for viewing sessions on Friday evenings. They invite visitors and university astronomy students inside the red-lit dome and up the metal stairs to the viewing platform. They select phenomena to observe and explain. Depending on the evening, they may point out the moon, other planets, constellations, or star clusters—anything they can see that's sufficiently bright to contend with the city's light pollution.

Graduate students and professors use the telescope to chart super giants and Barnard's Star, a red dwarf six light-years away from Earth—all of which they eagerly explain to observatory visitors.

UNIVERSITY OF NEW MEXICO CAMPUS OBSERVATORY

What: Off-the-beaten-path observatory

Where: 800 Yale Blvd. NE

Cost: None

Pro Tip: Viewing sessions are offered Friday evenings, 7-9 p.m. during Daylight Saving Time and 8-10 p.m. during Standard Time. Visitors may come and go as they please. It's advisable to call the observatory the day you intend to visit to ensure the viewing session will occur as planned.

The University of New Mexico Campus Observatory opens its dome for public viewings every Friday. **Photos** by Nick Cessac.

The University of New Mexico Campus Observatory offers special events in the case of solar eclipses.

MARTINEZTOWN MONUMENT

Where can you see a historic acequia near downtown?

Acequias (community-overseen irrigation canals) are usually thought of as agricultural landmarks, so how did one end up near downtown Albuquerque?

Martineztown's Acequia Madre was once far flung. Like many Albuquerque neighborhoods, Martineztown began as a separate village. In the Spanish Colonial period, Old Town settlers ventured three miles east to graze their livestock. In the 1830s, these pastures became farmland with the arrival of an acequia that cut from the Acequia de los Candelarias y Griegos north/south through Martineztown. For fifty years, the canal channeled water to the neighborhood.

In the 1880s, it was covered over with masonry and turned into an underground canal to enable new development in the downtown area and Martineztown. In the mid-twentieth century, developers filled in the acequia with dirt to make way for commercial buildings and residences along its path.

Martineztown sits along the original path of congressionally designated El Camino Real de Tierra Adentro National Historic Trail, a Spanish Colonial–era trading route between Mexico City and Santa Fe.

The Acequia Madre's former crossing testifies to Martineztown's early days in the 1830s. Photo by Ashley M. Biggers.

ACEQUIA MADRE

What: Historic irrigation canal

Where: West of the intersection of Edith Boulevard and Roma Avenue

Cost: None

Pro Tip: While you're there, don't miss the *Southwest Pieta*, also at Martineztown Park.

Some vestiges of the acequia stand today. It's marked with a xeri- and hardscaped pocket park across from Martineztown Park. The park honors the neighborhood's history, from its 1800s founding by Manuel and Anna Maria Martin to today. The neighborhood is bordered by Broadway Boulevard, I-25, Dr. Martin Luther King Jr. Avenue, and Mountain Road.

WINGING IT

What's Albuquerque's version of Cadillac Ranch?

Amarillo, Texas, has Cadillac Ranch, an art installation where ten cars are buried upright in the desert floor. Albuquerque has *Auto Hawk*, a winged creature made of reclaimed doors visible from Lead Avenue where it passes over First Street.

Sculptor Christopher Fennell's engineering background informs how he shapes materials. His work always incorporates discarded or found objects. For *Auto Hawk*, Fennell drew inspiration from Albuquerque hikes; he watched birds of prey glide along the Sandia Mountains' air currents when he lived in the Duke City from 2001 to 2003. He salvaged thirty doors from Birmingham, Alabama, where the artist currently lives, to build the towering hawk in flight. The finished piece is twenty-four feet tall.

The choice of car doors was fitting for the finished piece's location against a parking garage. "Having been a mechanical engineer, it was easy for me to pick a local structural engineer's brain to figure out the best way to frame the inside of the hawk and make it look like it is attached to the parking deck wall," Fennell says. "I like the idea of a parking deck's icon being a hawk made of car doors, all the car doors unique, like the drivers."

Albuquerque has a penchant for auto-related art. One of the city's most popular photo ops is at *Cruising San Mateo I*, made of a 1954 Chevy perched on a twenty-six-foot-high arch.

Auto Hawk *is built of thirty salvaged car doors*. Photo by Nick Cessac.

AUTO HAWK

What: Sculpture made of car doors

Where: 331 First St. SW

Cost: None

Pro Tip: For more Albuquerque public art, visit cabq.gov/culturalservices/public-art/public-art-in-albuquerque/interactive-public-art-map.

OUR LADY OF THE TREE

Why does an Old Town tree have a carving of Our Lady of Guadalupe?

Albuquerqueans and visitors passing the cottonwood stump at the corner of San Felipe de Neri church's grounds may spot a face emerging from the wood. But how did this carving get there?

Toby Avila, a parishioner of San Felipe de Neri, served in the U.S. Navy during the Korean conflict. During his deployment he prayed to Our Lady of Guadalupe, vowing that if he returned safely, he would show his appreciation. Back in Albuquerque, he began fulfilling his promise in 1958. He carved the figure of the Blessed Virgin in a cottonwood tree behind the church. He had a day job, so he carved only at night, using a flashlight to illuminate the figure as it slowly emerged from the wood. He employed a kitchen knife, sharpening stone, and mallet to create his version of the Blessed Virgin, which wears a blue mantilla and a golden crown. It took him more than a year to carve the tribute. Just a few days later, Avila died. Local legend says he still had blue paint on his fingertips when he lay in repose at his memorial service.

In 2011, a windstorm toppled the tree containing the carving. No one, including the carving, was harmed, which only increased the feeling of mysticism around the carving.

> **TREE CARVING**
>
> **What:** Our Lady of Guadalupe
>
> **Where:** San Felipe de Neri Church, 2005 N. Plaza NW
>
> **Cost:** None
>
> **Pro Tip:** This is a popular Instagram spot.

The Our Lady of Guadalupe in a cottonwood tree is an oft-seen sight in Old Town, but few know the story behind its carver. Photos by Ashley M. Biggers.

The church preserved the cottonwood tree stump in which the carving appears and has since relocated it to the front gardens.

The San Felipe de Neri parish dates back more than three hundred years.

SETTLERS AND SOPAIPILLAS

Where can you dine in one of Albuquerque's earliest buildings?

Church Street Café is housed in Casa de Ruiz (the house of Ruiz), which was built during the founding of Albuquerque. The Ruiz family constructed their adobe home shortly after 1706, which makes it one of the oldest residences in Albuquerque and among the oldest Spanish Colonial structures in New Mexico. In some places the walls are more than two feet thick, testifying to the structure's age as it was re-mudded and repaired over the years. It was built in the hacienda-style, in a U shape, and it was largely original until a 1920 flood washed away half the home and required rebuilding.

Beyond family anecdotes, the earliest formal records of the home can be traced to Julianna Lucero and Francisco Ruiz, around 1834. Their daughter, Sarah, was born in 1880. She passed the home along to Rufina G. Ruiz, who was the last of the Ruiz family to inhabit the home. When Rufina passed away at the age of ninety-one in 1991, the building was sold and converted into Church Street Café.

Sarah Ruiz may never have left the house she grew up in. Coleman believes the previous owner's spirit may linger in the home, turning on light switches and moving small figures in a Christmas nativity scene.

Church Street Café is housed in one of Albuquerque's earliest buildings just off Old Town Plaza, behind San Felipe de Neri church. Photo by Nick Cessac.

CHURCH STREET CAFÉ

What: Historic home turned restaurant

Where: 2111 Church St. NW

Cost: None

Pro Tip: Try the green-chile posole. The traditional New Mexican stew made with hominy is usually made with red chile, so this is a unique dish.

Marie Coleman, Church Street Café's owner, purchased the building and opened a restaurant as much because of her love of history as her love of the restaurant business. Coleman based her menu on her aunt's recipes, so the restaurant still has a homey feel—albeit a much different home than the Ruiz family compound in Albuquerque's founding years.

HIGH NOTES

How is Puccini connected to an Albuquerque theater?

Giacomo Puccini, one of the greatest composers of Italian opera, was rumored to be traveling to the West in 1913. Iole Bachechi, daughter of Oreste and Maria Bachechi, sought out the famous Puccini on the train. She found a Puccini, but not the famous composer. She instead connected with his cousin, Luigi Puccini, a journalist. Despite the case of mistaken identity, the two fell in love and were married in 1914. While the Bachechis went on to build the KiMo Theatre in 1927, Luigi built the Puccini Building. At various points in its history, it served as a grocery store, paint store, lamp store, and saloon.

In 1941, Joseph B. Burwinkle folded the Puccini Building into El Rey Theater, which became a popular movie theater and bar. It closed in the 1970s. In 1981, Virginia Puccini Doyle and Adelina Puccini Timofeyew, daughters of Luigi and Iole, turned it into a nightclub. It's now under new ownership as a live music venue. Even if the building wasn't founded by *the* Puccini, you'd expect the composer would be pleased that a building with a familial connection is devoted to music.

El Rey Theater has put considerable effort into restoring its neon sign, which faces Route 66.

HISTORIC EL REY THEATER

What: Historic theater

Where: 622 Central Ave. SW

Cost: None

Pro Tip: Bands in every genre, from hip hop to folk, play El Rey.

El Rey Theater was founded by Puccini—just not that *Puccini*. Photos by Ashley M. Biggers.

SOURCES

1. Good Times and Ghosts?
Site visit and interview with Jesse Herron, April 12, 2019.

2. Barely a Dent
"Broken Arrow Accidents." Atomic Heritage Foundation. https://www.atomicheritage.org/history/broken-arrow-accidents; interview with Jim Walther, director, National Museum of Nuclear Science & History, February 19, 2019; site visit, April 19, 2019.

3. A Bit of Blocking
Interview and site visit with Sara Dell, congregation member of First Unitarian Church and chairperson of the team that moved the Girard mural, August 2, 2019.

4. RIP: Gomez, Adrian
"'Breaking Bad' fan group places paid obituary for Walter White." *Albuquerque Journal*, 3 October 2013. https://www.abqjournal.com/275038/it-provides-closure.html; Lohmann, Patrick. "Hundreds of mourners bid farewell to Walter White." *Albuquerque Journal*, 20 October 2013. https://www.abqjournal.com/284998/hundreds-of-mourners-bid-farewell-to-walter-white.html; Lohmann, Patrick. "Walter White headstone to remain at Vernon's Steakhouse." *Albuquerque Journal*, 23 October 2013. https://www.abqjournal.com/286784/walter-headstone-to-stay-at-eatery.html.

5. A Curious Wavelength
Reed Jr., Ollie. "X-Rays, inside out." *Albuquerque Journal*, 27 September 2015. https://www.abqjournal.com/650085/inside.html; site visit and interview with Greg Morrison, executive director, March 1, 2019.

6. Early 911
"Village of Columbus and Camp Furlong, Columbus, New Mexico." National Park Service. https://www.nps.gov/nr/travel/american_latino_heritage/Village_of_Columbus_and_Camp_Furlong.html; site visit and interview with Tom Baker, owner, Telephone Museum of New Mexico, April 19, 2019.

7. Riding in Style
Interview with Jim Walther, director, National Museum of Nuclear Science & History, February 19, 2019; site visit, April 19, 2019.

8. Box Top Tales
Barber, Christine. "Spies Like Us." *New Mexico Magazine*. October 2009; Ripp, Bart. "Atom bomb secrets changed hands on High Street." *The Albuquerque Tribune*, 8 February 1985; site visit and interview with Steve Grant, owner, Downtown Historic Bed & Breakfast, June 27, 2019.

9. Press Pass
"The Albuquerque Press Club: History of Our Clubhouse." Site visit and interview with Laura Dunagan, president and membership chair, Albuquerque Press Club, March 2, 2019.

10. Cultural Gold
Site visit and interview with Elisabeth Stone, executive director, Gutierrez-Hubbell House, April 19, 2019.

11. Beneath the Surface
Site visit and interview with Dr. Matthew Schmader, archaeologist.

12. Off the Main Trail
Interview with Susanna Villanueva, park ranger, Visitor Services Division, April 1, 2019; Petroglyphs National Monument, https://www.nps.gov/petr; site visit with Steve Richey, trail patrol volunteer, April 11, 2019.

13. Does Not Compute
Kelly, Leslie. "Microsoft Cofounder Paul Allen Loved This Humble Café in Albuquerque." *Forbes*, 11 January 2019. https://www.forbes.com/sites/lesliekelly/2019/01/11/microsoft-co-founder-paul-allen-loved-this-humble-cafe-in-albuquerque/#5350e0483927; "Route 66 Sundowner Motel Renovated." City of Albuquerque. https://www.cabq.gov/family/what-were-doing/work-force-housing-sundowner-article/route-66-sundowner-motel-renovated; "This Day: Microsoft Founded." History. 27 July 2019. https://www.history.com/this-day-in-history/microsoft-founded.

14. The Secret Gate
Held, E. B. *A Spy's Guide to Santa Fe and Albuquerque*. Albuquerque, New Mexico: University of New Mexico Press, 2011.

15. The First Ascension
Albuquerque Historical Society Downtown Walking Tour, November 17, 2018; Albuquerque International Balloon Fiesta Heritage Committee. *Images of Modern America: Albuquerque International Balloon Fiesta*. Charleston, South Carolina: Arcadia Publishing, 2016.

16. Albuquerque's "Beach"
Schmader, Matt. *Images of America: Albuquerque's Parks and Open Space*. Charleston, South Carolina: Arcadia Publishing, 2011.

17. Let's Get Physical
Interview with William R. Lovelace's niece Mary Ann Bunten, July 22, 2019; International Space Hall of Fame at the New Mexico Museum of Space History, William R. Lovelace II. http://www.nmspacemuseum.org/halloffame/detail.php?id=19; Page, Joseph T. *Images of America: New Mexico Space Trail*. Charleston, South Carolina: Arcadia Publishing, 2013.

18. Glass Garden
Interview with forestry supervisor Matthew Peterson, June 20, 2019; site visit, July 26, 2019.

19. Well, Shoot
Ausherman, Stephen. *Walking Albuquerque: 30 Tours of the Duke City's Historic Neighborhoods, Ditch Trails, Urban Nature, and Public Art*. Berkeley, California: Wilderness Press, 2015; Bannerman, Ty. *Images of America: Forgotten Albuquerque*. Charleston, South Carolina: Arcadia Press, 2009; Peters, Joey. "Why one advocate says Old Town Confederate flag removal isn't enough." *New Mexico Political Report*, 19 August 2015. https://nmpoliticalreport.com/2015/08/19/why-one-advocate-says-old-town-confederate-flag-removal-isnt-enough; Reed Jr., Ollie. "'We need to remember our history.'" *Albuquerque Journal*, 26 July 2015. https://www.abqjournal.com/618370/we-need-to-remember-our-history.html; Steinberg, David. "Major Teel's War." *Albuquerque Journal*, 19 February 2012. https://www.abqjournal.com/88996/major-teels.html.

20. Artistic Fossils
Albuquerque Metropolitan Arroyo Flood Control Authority. "Calabacillas Arroyo." http://www.amafca.org/projects/calabacillas.html; "Calabacillas Arroyo Flood Control, Open Space, and Art." http://www.amafca.org/documents/Calabacillas_Flyer.pdf; interview with Kevin Troutman, GIS manager, Albuquerque Metropolitan Arroyo Flood Control Authority, July 19, 2019; site visit, July 19, 2019.

21. Into the Stacks
Email interview with Dr. Lea S. McChesney, curator of ethnology, Maxwell Museum of Anthropology, August 1, 2019; interview and site visit with Dr. Carla Sinopoli, museum director, Maxwell Museum of Anthropology, July 19, 2019.

22. From the Fire
Atlas Obscura. Pueblo Montaño Chainsaw Sculpture Garden. https://www.atlasobscura.com/places/pueblo-montano-chainsaw-sculpture-garden?utm_source=atlas-forum&utm_medium=referral; Open Space Alliance. Pueblo Montaño Picnic Area & Sculpture Park. http://openspacealliance.org/where-is-open-space/bosque-north-destinations/pueblo-montano-picnic-area-sculpture-park.

23. Thorny Frosty
Atlas Obscura. "Tumbleweed Snowman." https://www.atlasobscura.com/places/tumbleweed-snowman; interview with Kevin Troutman, GIS manager, Albuquerque Metropolitan Arroyo Flood Control Authority, September 11, 2019.

24. Rolling Along
Marking Time: The Center of the City Project. Albuquerque Public Art. https://vimeo.com/51760982; site visit and interview with Leba Freed, executive director, September 5, 2019.

25. Nah, I'm Gonna Stay at the Disco
Class, July 26, 2019; interview with Ashley Fathergill, September 12, 2019.

26. Card Reader
Interview with Oma, August 24, 2019; Staff. "Is a Rail Yards visit in the cards?" *Albuquerque Journal*, 17 August 2015. https://www.abqjournal.com/629446/is-a-rail-yards-visit-in-the-cards.html.

27. Gotcha Day
Interview with Ellen Babcock, 2017.

28. With Thanks
Site visit, September 14, 2019.

29. Family Farmers
Site visit and interview with Chantelle Wagner, September 15, 2019.

30. Flying High
Bisharat, Andrew. "After Crossing Pacific, Record-Setting Balloonists Land off Baja Coast." *National Geographic*, 31 January 2015. https://www.nationalgeographic.com/news/2015/1/150130-balloon-pacific-ocean-helium-gas-japan-new-mexico; "Troy Bradley." National Balloon Museum. https://www.nationalballoonmuseum.com/wp-content/uploads/2017/06/Troy-Bradley.pdf; site visit, September 14, 2019.

31. Layer by Layer
Jaffe, Matthew. "The Passion of Frederico Vigil." *Sunset Magazine*, October 2005. https://www.sunset.com/travel/southwest/passion-of-frederico-vigil; Visit Albuquerque. "New Mexico Artist Frederico Vigil to Embark on a Four-Year Fresco Project at the Convention Center." https://www.visitalbuquerque.org/articles/post/new-mexico-artist-frederico-vigil-to-embark-on-a-four-year-fresco-project-at-the-convention-center; site visit, September 14, 2019.

32. Sun Powered
Hood, Taylor. "The Solar Building." *Albuquerque the Magazine*, July 2019; interview with Thea Haver, director, and Ethan Aronson, director of guest experience, Modern Albuquerque, June 14, 2019; Sawyer, Simon. "Solar Building." Albuquerque Modernism. http://albuquerquemodernism.unm.edu/wp/solar-building.

33. Torpedo Tributes
Staff. "Submariners Commemorate Sinking of USS Bullhead." *Albuquerque Journal*, 5 August 2010. https://www.abqjournal.com/8745/submariners-commemorate-sinking-of-uss-bullhead.html; site visit, September 14, 2019.

34. No Longer Starving Artists
Armijo, Barbara. "Downtown Tortilla Factory Out of Business After 30 Years." *Albuquerque Journal*, 10 June 2004. https://www.abqjournal.com/news/metro/184296metro06-10-04.htm; crider, sheri. Sanitary Tortilla

Factory. sanitarytortillafactory.org; interview with sheri crider, September 11, 2019.

35. Blue Plate Special
Email interview with Matt DiGregory, CEO, Home on the Range, Inc., September 16, 2019; site visit, September 20, 2019.

36. Anthropological Hijinks
Bannerman, Ty. "Enter Sandia Man: Revisiting the Site of a 20th Century Archaeological Scandal." *Atlas Obscura*, 17 February 2006. https://www.atlasobscura.com/articles/enter-sandia-man-revisiting-the-site-of-a-20th-century-archeological-scandal; Preston, Douglas. "The Mystery of Sandia Cave." *The New Yorker*, 12 June 1995, 66; Sandia Man Cave and Trailhead. Cibola National Forest. https://www.fs.usda.gov/recarea/cibola/recarea/?recid=71221; site visit, August 25, 2019; Jessica C. Thompson, Nawa Sugiyama and Gary S. Morgan. "Taphonomic Analysis of the Mammalian Fauna from Sandia Cave, New Mexico, and the 'Sandia Man' Controversy." *American Antiquity*, Vol. 73, No. 2 (April, 2008), 337-360. https://www.jstor.org/stable/25470481?seq=1#page_scan_tab_contents.

37. Still Standing
Interview with Joe Sabatini, member of Albuquerque Historical Society's speaker bureau and Indian Pueblo Cultural Center volunteer, August 13, 2019; Palmer, Mo. "Albuquerque Indian School." Albuquerque Historical Society. http://www.historicabq.org/albuquerque-indian-school.html; Palmer, Mo. "Indian School Dormitory and Club." Albuquerque Historical Society. https://www.historicabq.org/indian-school-dormitory-and-club.html.

38. Before the Brand
Nathanson, Rick. "Hotel Andaluz returns to its roots." *Albuquerque Journal*. 19 April 2019. https://www.abqjournal.com/1305003/hotel-andaluz-returns-to-its-roots.html; "Our Story." Hotel Andaluz. https://hotelandaluz.com/our-story.

39. Motor Lodge Mural
"De Anza Motor Lodge, Albuquerque, New Mexico." National Park Service. https://www.nps.gov/nr/travel/route66/de_anza_motor_lodge_albuquerque.html; site visit and interview with Jim Trump, president of Strategic Asset Management and construction manager of the mixed-use redevelop¬ment, July 17, 2019.

40. Midas's Tower
Murphy, Alexa. "Case Study: First National Bank Building East." Albuquerque Modernism. http://albuquerquemodernism.unm.edu/wp/first-national-bank-building; interview with Thea Haver, director, and Ethan Aronson, director of guest experience, Modern Albuquerque, June 14, 2019.

41. Four-Way Stop
Albuquerque Historical Society Downtown Walking Tour, November 17,

2018; "The History of Route 66." National Historic Route 66 Federation. https://www.national66.org/history-of-route-66; "The History of Route 66." The Route-66. https://www.theroute-66.com/santa-fe-loop.html.

42. Giddy Up
Interview with Roland Penttila, Albuquerque Historical Society, August 13, 2019; site visit, August 8, 2019.

43. Fit for a Princess
Interview with Thea Haver, director, and Ethan Aronson, director of guest experience, Modern Albuquerque, June 14, 2019; Townsend, Cameron. "Case Study: Princess Jeanne Park." Modern Albuquerque. http://albuquerquemodernism.unm.edu/wp/princess-jeanne-park-albuquerque-nm.

44. Mile Markers
Marking Time: The Center of the City Project. Albuquerque Public Art. https://vimeo.com/51760982.

45. Where's Aldo?
Aldo Leopold Neighborhood Historic District. Living Places. https://www.livingplaces.com/NM/Bernalillo_County/Albuquerque_City/Aldo_Leopold_Neighborhood_Historic_District.html; *History of Albuquerque's Open Space*. City of Albuquerque GOVTV. https://www.youtube.com/watch?v=Ev1L5DhaKDQ&t=315s.

46. Timber!
Nathanson, Rick. "Nothing says 'good eats' like a giant lumberjack." *Albuquerque Journal*, 11 June 2019. https://www.abqjournal.com/1326739/nothing-says-good-eats-like-a-giant-lumberjack.html; "Paul Bunyan." Albuquerque Daily Photo. https://albuquerquedailyphoto.com/paul-bunyan.

47. A New Twist
Email interview with Bart Prince, September 18, 2019.

48. Creative Spaces
"Albuquerque Artist Rooms." Nativo Lodge. https://www.nativolodge.com/artist-rooms; interview with Cloudface, mural artist, February 25, 2019; interview with Rhett Lynch, mural artist, February 26, 2019; site visit, June 28, 2017.

49. Artistic Intent
Johnson, Patricia C. "Houston sculptor's project led to his death." *Houston Chronicle*, 15 June 2006. https://www.chron.com/entertainment/article/Houston-sculptor-s-project-led-to-his-death-1553982.php; Navrot, Miguel. "Luis Jimenez Jr. Killed: Statuary Pinned Sculptor." *Albuquerque Journal*, 14 June 2006. https://www.abqjournal.com/news/state/468202nm06-14-06.htm; site visit, August 8, 2019.

50. A Side of Hope
Interview with Julie Yung, manager, Hope Café, HopeWorks, August 29, 2019; interview with Greg Morris, executive director, HopeWorks, August 27, 2019; site visit, August 26, 2019.

51. Go with the Flow
Interview with Kevin Troutman, September 13, 2019; site visit, September 20, 2019.

52. Art Hub
Conde, Clark. "Finding the Words that Heal." *The Weekly Alibi*, 5 September 2019. https://alibi.com/art/59250/Finding-the-Words-That-Heal.html?fbclid=IwAR1z7A3IldUUfualQ6kDbrevcbAXGjmZOTh6a7RdgwRdyhl-UTWSEE71rMg; Inez Guzmán, Alicia. "Get Cultured." *New Mexico Magazine*, June 2019. https://www.newmexico.org/nmmagazine/articles/post/el-chante; site visit and interview with Bianca Encinias and Manuel Gonzalez, 2018.

53. No Big Gulps Here
"Historic Landmarks." City of Albuquerque. https://www.cabq.gov/planning/boards-commissions/landmarks-commission/historic-landmarks.

54. Altered States
Tour and interview with Larry D. Parker, KiMo Theatre manager, August 21, 2019.

55. You're Going to Need More Clamps for That
"ATLAS-I." *Atlas Obscura*. https://www.atlasobscura.com/places/atlas-i; Reuben, Charles. "Empire My Prince: Carl Baum, trestle-maker." *The Weekly Alibi*, 6 January 2011. https://alibi.com/news/35291/Empire-My-Prince.html.

56. To the Wall
Site visit and interview with Janet deVesty, executive director, Unser Racing Museum, August 22, 2019.

57. Written in Stone
Interview with Dr. David Eck, state trust archaeologist, September 23, 2019; "Mystery Stone, Valencia County." New Mexico State Land Office. http://www.nmstatelands.org/great-recreational-areas.aspx.

58. Skating Along
Interview with Katie Jurney, Albuquerque Roller Derby League skater, September 12, 2019; site visit, September 21, 2019.

59. Movie Memories
Site visit and interview with Hugh Hacket, owner, September 20, 2019.

60. A Suburb of One's Own
Interview with Brenda Dabney, ancestor of Henry Outley, September 20,

2019; Snyder, Christy; Glanzberg, Joel; Mang, Nicolas. "The International District, Albuquerque, New Mexico." *Story of Place Institute*. December 2015. https://www.cabq.gov/culturalservices/public-art/documents/02-idreport_storyofplace_booklet.pdf; Tate, Van. "Hidden Histories: East End Addition becomes Albuquerque's first African-American suburb." KRQE. 15 January 2018. https://www.youtube.com/watch?v=QqiVw5mLD1Q.

61. Coming Home
Staff. "George Morrison (Jim's Dad) Dies at 89." *Albuquerque Journal*, 12 December 2008. https://www.abqjournal.com/17935/150pm-george-morrison-jims-dad-dies-at-89.html; Associated Press. "Fans push to preserve Jim Morrison's New Mexico home." *Albuquerque Journal*, 5 May 2015. https://www.abqjournal.com/579898/fans-push-to-preserve-jim-morrisons-albuquerque-home.html; "Jim Morrison's Childhood Home." KOAT, 29 April 2015. https://www.youtube.com/watch?v=l7bz61fib_8.

62. Cheers to Prohibition
"Oldest Bar in Albuquerque—Silva's Saloon, Bernalillo, NM." Bucket List Bars. https://www.youtube.com/watch?v=qNHQptYev7I; Lanier, Clint, and Hembree, Derek. "From Bootlegging to Respectable, Silva's Saloon, Bernalillo, New Mexico." *Huffington Post*, 2 October 2013. https://www.huffpost.com/entry/silvas-saloon-new-mexico_b_4010413; site visit, September 16, 2019.

63. A Sight to Behold
Coltrin, Mike. *Sandia Mountain Hiking Guide, Revised and Expanded Edition*. Albuquerque, New Mexico: University of New Mexico Press, 2019; site visit, September 22, 2019.

64. Gone but Not Forgotten
"Back to Life: The Community of Historic Fairview Cemetery: Excerpts from an exhibit at Albuquerque Museum." Albuquerque Historical Society. http://www.historicabq.org/fairview-cemetery-exhibit.html; Bannerman, Ty. "The Land of the Dead." *The Weekly Alibi*, 6 November 2014. https://alibi.com/feature/48039/The-Land-of-the-Dead.html; Briseño, Elaine. "Cemeteries, like Albuquerque's Fairview, tell a community's story." *Albuquerque Journal*, 28 August 2016. https://www.abqjournal.com/834346/grave-impressions.html; Reed, Ollie, Jr. "Courage Under Fire." *Albuquerque Journal*, 9 June 2019; Schwartz, Susan. "Historic Fairview Memorial Park." Albuquerque Historical Society. http://www.historicabq.org/fairview-memorial-park.html.

65. Parq It
Cassyle Carr, Jessica. "A Dose of History." *The Weekly Alibi*, 8 November 2010. https://alibi.com/news/34721/A-Dose-of-History.html; Hider, Anna. "This swanky boutique hotel has a dark secret—it was once a psychiatric hospital!" *Roadtrippers*, January 2016. https://maps.roadtrippers.com/stories/this-swanky-boutique-hotel-has-a-dark-secret-it-was-once-a-psychiatric-hospital; "Top 9 Most Haunted Hotels in New Mexico." Haunted Rooms. https://www.hauntedrooms.com/product/hotel-parq-central-

albuquerque-new-mexico. Quigley, Winthrop. "Memorial Hospital Being Closed." *Albuquerque Journal*, 6 March 2007. https://www.abqjournal.com/biz/543780business03-06-07.htm.

66. Stuffed
"Eating Big." KOAT. https://www.facebook.com/watch/?v=521614754967817; Garduño, Gil. "K&I Diner – Albuquerque, New Mexico." Gil's Thrilling (and Filling) Blog, 9 May 2019. https://www.nmgastronome.com/?p=306.

67. Craning to See
Site visit and interview with Natalie Padilla, September 20, 2019.

68. Burgers and Thrift Store Finds
Site visit and interview with Phil Chavez, owner, September 19, 2019.

69. Going Green
De Chant, Tim. Per Square Mile. https://persquaremile.com/2011/01/27/parkland-per-person-in-the-united-states; History of Albuquerque's Open Space. City of Albuquerque GOVTV. https://www.youtube.com/watch?v=Ev1L5DhaKDQ&t=315s; interview with Philip Clelland, Public Information Office, Albuquerque Parks and Recreation Department, September 19, 2019.

70. Glass House
"Our Story." Tinkertown Museum. http://tinkertown.com/?page_id=2; "Tinkertown." Roadside America. https://www.roadsideamerica.com/story/11018; site visit, September 20, 2019.

71. Forgotten Village
"Prehistoric Background: Tijeras Pueblo Archaeological Site." Friends of the Tijeras Pueblo. http://www.friendsoftijeraspueblo.org/siteoriginshistory.html; site visit, September 20, 2019.

72. Mountain Memorial
Coltrin, Mike. *Sandia Mountain Hiking Guide, Revised and Expanded Edition*. Albuquerque, New Mexico: University of New Mexico Press, 2019; Smith, Toby. "Remembering TWA 260: Man on a Mission to Keep Memory Alive." *Albuquerque Journal*, 13 February 2005. https://www.abqjournal.com/news/metro/304338metro02-13-05.htm; "TWA Flight 260 Crash Site." Atlas Obscura. https://www.atlasobscura.com/places/twa-crash-site; Williams, Charles M. "The Crash of TWA Flight 260." Albuquerque, New Mexico: University of New Mexico Press, 2010.

73. Math Aloft
Email interview with Jonathan Wolfe, executive director, Fractal Foundation, September 15, 2019.

74. Taco Tuesdays, Sopaipilla Saturdays
Chavez, Barbara. "Restaurant's Lenten Specialties Rich in Tradition, History." *Albuquerque Journal*, 27 March 2002. https://www.abqjournal.

com/food/637132food03-27-02.htm; Garduño, Gil. "Abuelita's New Mexican Kitchen – Bernalillo and Albuquerque, New Mexico." Gil's Thrilling (and Filling) Blog, 1 August 2019. https://www.nmgastronome.com/?p=126.

75. Slithering Sights
Nelson, Kate. "The Story Behind Those Huge Snakes." *New Mexico Magazine*, July 2019. https://www.newmexico.org/nmmagazine/articles/post/the-snakes-of-mesa-del-sol.

76. Loco for Locomotives
Site visit and interview with Mike Hartshorne, president, New Mexico Steam Locomotive & Railroad Historical Society, August 24, 2019.

77. Puck Drop
Interview with Trevor Flint, general manager, Outpost Ice Arenas, September 12, 2019; site visit, September 27, 2019.

78. Duke City's Doge
"2017 Architectural Tour: A Toast to Trost." New Mexico Architectural Foundation. https://newmexico-architecturalfoundation.org/2017/09/25/2017tour-trost; Carr, Jessica Cassyle. "Renaissance of Resilience: Occidental Life Building at 100." *The Weekly Alibi*, 14 December 2017. https://alibi.com/news/54796/Renaissance-of-Resilience.html; "Historic Landmarks." Albuquerque Planning Commission. https://www.cabq.gov/planning/boards-commissions/landmarks-commission/historic-landmarks.

79. Cultural Nexus
Staff. "Blue Smokehouse Brings Nexus Home." *Albuquerque Journal*, 18 March 2019. https://www.abqjournal.com/1293129/nambeacute-opens-store-on-west-side.html; email interview with Cathryn McGill, June 6, 2019; site visit and interview with Johnny Goodwin, Navajo Elks Lodge member, June 21, 2019.

80. A Different Kind of Cleanse
Site visit and interview with Michael O. Wieclaw, June 28, 2018.

81. That's a Stretch
Mine Shaft Tavern. https://www.themineshafttavern.com; site visit, September 28, 2019; Snyder, Gail. "The One and Only Mine Shaft Tavern." *Local Flavor*, 4 May 2015. http://www.localflavormagazine.com/the-one-and-only-mine-shaft-tavern.

82. Chiseling History
Art and Architecture Tour, September 14, 2019.

83. Lucy, We've Got a Star
Ausherman, Stephen. *Walking Albuquerque: 30 Tours of the Duke City's Historic Neighborhoods, Ditch Trails, Urban Nature, and Public Art*. Berkeley, California: Wilderness Press, 2015; Lawrence, Kristi D.

"Loving Vivian Vance: The highs and lows of an Albuquerque legend." *The Weekly Alibi*, 27 March 2014. https://alibi.com/art/46548/Loving-Vivian-Vance.html; Roberts, Kathaleen. "ABQ Museum has a Vivian Vance exhibit." *Albuquerque Journal*, 23 March 2014. https://www.abqjournal.com/373077/abq-museum-has-vivian-vance-exhibit.html; Roberts, Kathaleen. "Vivian Vance's sister shares her memories of the 'I Love Lucy' star." *Albuquerque Journal*, 7 September 2014. https://www.abqjournal.com/458139/sister-remembers-actor-vivian-vance.html.

84. Generations of Genízaro
Gonzales, Moises, and Lamadrid, Enrique R. (Eds.). *Nación Genízara: Ethnogenesis, Place, and Identity in New Mexico*. Albuquerque, New Mexico: University of New Mexico Press, Fall 2019; Gonzales, Moises. "The Genízaro Land Grant Settlements of New Mexico." *Journal of the Southwest*, 56, 4 (Winter 2014), 583-602.

85. Universal Views
Interview with Ylva Pihlström, professor, Department of Physics and Astronomy, University of New Mexico, September 12, 2019; site visit, September 27, 2019.

86. Martineztown Monument
Sanchez, Joseph P., and Miller, Larry D. *Martineztown 1823-1950: Hispanics, Italians, Jesuits & Land Investors in New Town Albuquerque*. Albuquerque, New Mexico: Rio Grande Books, 2009.

87. Winging It
Email interview with Christopher Fennell, September 28, 2019.

88. Our Lady of the Tree
Associated Press. "Storm topples tree but religious icon survives." 4 December 2011. http://www.rdrnews.com/archive/?p=39946; Lowe, Sam. *New Mexico Curiosities: Quirky Characters, Roadside Oddities & Other Offbeat Stuff*. Guilford, Connecticut: Globe Pequot, 2009.

89. Settlers and Sopaipillas
"About the Café." Church Street Café. https://www.churchstreetcafe.com/about-the-cafe.html; Ausherman, Stephen. *Walking Albuquerque: 30 Tours of the Duke City's Historic Neighborhoods, Ditch Trails, Urban Nature, and Public Art*. Berkeley, California: Wilderness Press, 2015; interview with Marie Coleman, August 23, 2018.

90. High Notes
"Historic Buildings Inventory Walking Tour." The Arts & Cultural District. http://www.downtownacd.org/wp-content/uploads/2013/08/acd-historic-inventory2.pdf.

INDEX

40 & 8 boxcars, 56–57
Abuelita's New Mexican Kitchen, 166–167
acequias, 190
Albuquerque box, 31
Albuquerque Convention Center, 62–63
Albuquerque Country Club, 32
Albuquerque Indian School, 74–75
Albuquerque International Balloon Fiesta, 30, 115, 153, 164–165
Albuquerque Open Space, ix, 22, 24, 36, 85
Albuquerque Metropolitan Arroyo Flood Control Authority, 40, 46, 120
Albuquerque Press Club, ix, 18–19
Albuquerque Rail Yards, 48
Albuquerque Roller Derby, x, 134–135
"Alburquerque" trolley, 3
Allen, Paul, 26
Alvarado Hotel, 18, 49
AMAFCA volcano, 121
American Society of Radiologic Technologists, 10
Anderson Abruzzo International Balloon Museum, ix, 60–61
Arroyosaurus, 40–41
AT&SF 2926, 170–171
AT&T, 13
ATLAS-I, 128–129
Atchison, Topeka & Santa Fe Railway Hospital, 148
Auto Hawk, 192–193
Bachechi, Iole, 198
Bachechi, Maria, 198
Bachechi, Oreste, 126, 198

Baker, Tom, ix, 13
Ballou, Virginia Outley, 139
Baum, Dr. Carl E., 128
Baumann, Gustave, 182–183
Bellamah, Abdul Hamid "Dale," 104–105
Bernalillo, 21, 48, 71, 82, 142–143, 146, 167
Big Jim Farms, 58–59
Boller Brothers Architecture Company, 126
bosque, 33, 36, 44–45, 109
Box, Jennifer and Kevin, 152
Bradley, Troy, 60–61
Breaking Bad, 8–9, 70
Bridgers and Paxton Engineering, 64
Broadway Market Building, The, 184
Broken Arrows, 4–5
Brueggemann, Sherri, 106
Calabacillas Arroyo, 40–41
cannons, 38–39
Carnuel, 187
Carson, Ken, x, 176
Casa de Ruiz, 196
Casas de Suenos bed and breakfast, 112
Center of the City Project, 83, 106–107
Chavez, Mark, 44–45
Chavez, Phil, 154–155
Church Street Café, 196–197
City of Albuquerque, x, 23, 31–32, 49, 54, 67, 79, 106, 116, 156, 168, 170
Cliff's Amusement Park, 85

Cohen, Lona, 28
Coleman, Marie, 196–197
Columbus, New Mexico, 12
Confederates, 38
CooLLoop, 172
Coronado Park, 107, 170
Conservancy Beach, 32
crider, sheri, ix, 69
De Anza Motor Lodge, 78–79
Doge's Palace, 174–175
Downtown Growers Market, 52–53
Downtown Historic Bed & Breakfast, ix, 17
DiGregory, Matt, ix, 70–71
Duarte, Yamilette, 106
Dunagan, Laura, ix, 19
East End Addition, 138–139
Eck, David, x, 132–133
Edaakie, Tony, 78–79
El Camino Real de Tierra Adentro, 20, 190
El Chante: Casa de Cultura, 122–123
El Rey Theater, 198–199
El Vado Motel, 178
Expo New Mexico, 56–57, 135
Eye of the Sandias, 129, 144–145
Fairview Memorial Park, 146–147
Fathergill, Ashley, ix, 50–51
Fennell, Christopher, 192
Fibonacci, 164–165
First National Bank Building East, 80–81
First Unitarian Church, ix, 6–7
fractal hot-air balloons, 165
Fractal Foundation, x, 164–165
French Boxcar Committee, 56
fresco, 62–63
Friends of the Orphan Signs, ix, 54–55

Gates, Bill, 26–27
genízaro, 186–187
Girard, Alexander, 6–7
glass garden, 36–37
Gold, Harry, 16, 76
Gonzalez, Miguel, 123
Goodwin, Johnny, x, 176–177
Grandma's K&I Diner, 150–151
Grant, Steve and Kara, x, 17
Gratitude Train, The, 56–57
Greenglass, David, 16–17
Grill, The, 154–155
Gutiérrez-Hubbell House, ix, 20–21
Gutiérrez, Juliana, 20
Hall, Theodore, 28–29
Harper, William, 10–11
Herron, Jesse, 2–3
Hess, Kay, 150
Hibben, Dr. Frank, 42, 72–73, 132
Hilton, Conrad, 76–77
Hope Café, x, 118–119
HopeWorks, 118–119
Hoshour, Harvey, 6, 80
hot-air balloon, 30–31, 164–165
Hotel Andaluz, 77
Hotel Parq Central, 18, 148–149
Hubbell, Juan "Lorenzo," 20
Huning Highland neighborhood, 16
I Love Lucy, 184–185
Indian School Dormitory and Club, 74–75
Indianapolis 500, 130
Indianapolis Motor Speedway, 130–131
Infinitude, 164–165
Jimenez, Luis, 116–117
Jones Motor Company, 124
Kellys Brew Pub, 124–125
KGB, 28–29

KiMo Theatre, 126-127, 174, 198
Kirtland Air Force Base, 4, 66-67, 128-129, 140
La Quinta Cultural Center, 182
Leopold, Aldo, 32, 108-109
Little Beaver Town, 84-85
longest stand-up bar, 180-181
Los Matachines, 187
Los Poblanos Historic Inn and Organic Farm, 182-183
Lovelace Clinic, 35
Lovelace, William Randolph "Randy" II, 34-35, 139
lumberjack, 110-111
M&J Sanitary Tortilla Factory, 68-69
Madrid, 136, 180-181
Maggie's Diner, x, 136-137
maggot pit, 178-179
Manhattan Project, 14-16, 28, 76
Martineztown, 116, 190-191
Maxwell Museum of Anthropology, ix, 42-43
May Café, 110
McDuffie Park, 156-157
Media Arts Collaborative Charter School, 55
Mercury Seven, 34
Mercury Thirteen, 35
Metal The Shop, 178
Microsoft, 26-27
Mine Shaft Tavern, 180-181
MLLAD, 28-29
Morrison, Greg, ix, 11
Morrison, Jim, 140-141
Mystery Stone, 132-133
Navajo Elks Lodge, 176-177
NASA, 35
National Museum of Nuclear Science & History, 4, 14-15

National Register of Historic Places, 75, 79, 108
Native American Community Academy, 75
Nativo Lodge, 114-115
Nautilus, The, 112-113
New Mexico Ice Wolves, 172-173
New Mexico Steam Locomotive & Railroad Historical Society, 170
Nexus Blue Smokehouse, x, 176-177
Occidental Life Building, 174-175
Old Town, 30, 38-39, 48, 107, 116, 168, 190, 194-195, 197
Oppenheimer, J. Robert, 14-15
Oma, ix, 52-53
Origami in the Garden, 152-153
Our Lady of Guadalupe, 194-195
Outley, Henry, 138
Outpost Ice Arenas, 172-173
Painted Lady Bed & Brew, ix, 2-3
Parks, Susan, 12-13
Peterson, Matthew, ix, 36-37
Petroglyphs National Monument, ix, 23-24
Piedras Marcadas Canyon, 23-25
Piedras Marcadas Pueblo, ix, 22-23
Prince, Bart, x, 112-113
Princess Esmeralda, 52-53
Princess Jeanne Neighborhood, 104-105
Puccini, Giacomo, 198
Puccini, Luigi, 198
Pueblo-Deco architecture, 126-127
Pueblo Montaño Chainsaw Sculpture Garden, 45
Range Café, ix, 70-71
rattlesnakes, 168
Red Ryder, 84-85

Ross, Edmund G., 146
Route 66, 1, 26, 54, 78–80, 82–84, 124, 137, 142, 178, 184, 198
San Miguel de Loredo de Carnué, 187
San Felipe de Neri Church, 38, 194, 197
Sandia Man Cave, 72–73
Sandia Mountains, 1, 62, 72–73, 82, 129, 144, 147, 152, 162–163, 192
Schmader, Matthew, ix, 22–23
Shalako, 78
silent disco yoga, 50–51
Silva's Saloon, 142–143
Silva, Felix Sr., 142–143
Silva, Felix Jr., 142–143
Simms, Albert G., 147, 182
Simms, Ruth Hanna McCormick, 147, 182
Sirhan, Sirhan, 10
Smith Family Totem, 29, 43
Solar Building, 64–65
Southwest Pieta, 116–117, 191
Spy House, 16–17, 28, 41
storybook ranch homes, 104
Sundowner Motel, 26, 55
swastikas, 126
Teel, Trevanion T. (Major General), 38
Telephone Museum of New Mexico, x, 12–13
Tijeras Pueblo, 160–161
Tingley Beach, 32–33
Tingley, Clyde, 32–33, 77
Tinkertown Museum, 158–159
Tiukhtyaev, Leonid, 61
Tlowitsis Nation, 42–43

Trinity Test, 15, 29, 76
Trost, Henry C., 174
Tumbleweed Snowman, 46–47
TWA Flight 260, 162
Two Eagles, 60–61
U-PICK green chile farm, 58–59
University of New Mexico, 22, 28–29, 42, 73, 117, 133, 146, 160, 188–189
University of New Mexico Campus Observatory, 188–189
Unser, Al Jr., 130
Unser, Al Sr., 130
Unser Racing Museum, x, 131
USS Bullhead Memorial Park, 66–67
Van Tassel, Park, 30–31
Vance, Vivian, 184–185
Vernon's Speakeasy, 8–9
Vigil, Frederico, 62–63
Villa, Pancho, 12–13
Village Shops at Los Ranchos, The, 9
Wagner, Jim, 58
Wallace, C. G., 78–79
Ward, Ross, 158–159
Wieclaw, Michael O., 178
Wells Park neighborhood, 2
Wheels Museum, ix, 48–49
White, Walter, 8–9
Whittlesey, Charles, 18
Whittlesey House Preservation Foundation, 19
Wild Hogs, 136–137
Wolfe, Jonathan, x, 164
YogaZo, ix, 50–51